ANIMAL AMIGURUMI

ADVENTURES

VOLUME I

15 Crochet Patterns to Create
Adorable Amigurumi Critters

BY LAUREN ESPY

BLUE STAR
PRESS

DEDICATION

In memory of my sweet mom, Shannon. You always encouraged me
to go for my dreams and were my biggest cheerleader through it all.

TABLE OF CONTENTS

INTRODUCTION

Hello, friends! I'm so excited that you're here for this new amigurumi adventure!

My love for crochet started back in 2009 after my grandma gifted me a set of crochet hooks, yarn, and a book about amigurumi. Discovering I could make cute toys out of yarn and a hook fascinated me. I ended up teaching myself how to crochet with the help of some online videos, and after making my first project—a wonky-looking octopus—I was obsessed.

After getting the hang of how to make amigurumi and how to crochet different shapes, I started designing my own toys. Being able to sketch out a design and turn it into something physical will always be my favorite part of being a crochet designer. Seeing an item come to life is such a cool thing! In 2015, I finally opened my online shop, A Menagerie of Stitches, where I sell finished items as well as patterns for other crocheters to make their own amigurumi. Since then, I have published many more patterns and even wrote two books, *Whimsical Stitches* and *Crochet Cafe*. It's been so much fun to see everyone make amigurumi and fall in love with crochet after picking up my first two books.

For this book, I decided to explore a theme I haven't really dipped my toes into before, and that is the world of animals! Animals are amazing creatures and I loved getting to learn more about them as I crocheted each one.

Each chapter of this book contains five animals that can be found in different parts of the world. We begin our trek with a trip to the ocean to visit some clever clownfish and crabs. Next, we venture into the jungle to meet a curious sloth and a very talkative toucan. Then we take a hike through a forest and discover a fox and squirrel chatting.

As you navigate through this book, I hope you find your favorite animal or discover a few new ones to love. Customize them by choosing your favorite yarn colors or adding little embellishments. The possibilities are endless!

I'm ready for this next adventure and can't wait to take you all along with me. Pack your yarn and crochet hooks and let's go meet some seriously cute animals!

Happy crocheting!

Lauren

TOOLS & MATERIALS

YARN

There are many different types of yarns to choose from, but my favorite for amigurumi is a worsted weight acrylic. Worsted weight is referred to as a level 4, or medium weight yarn. I like using acrylic because it comes in lots of different colors, is affordable, and works great for making amigurumi. Choose your favorite brands and colors for the animals in this book!

For a list of the specific brands and exact colors I used throughout this book, please visit my website, www.amenagerieofstitchesblog.com

CROCHET HOOK

Crochet hooks come in a variety of sizes and can be made from aluminum, plastic, or wood. I typically grab an aluminum hook with an ergonomic handle, as this feels best in my hand while crocheting. Make sure to pick a hook that works and feels comfortable in your hand.

To keep it simple, all the patterns in this book will use a F/3.75mm crochet hook. Of course, you may choose to use a larger or smaller hook, if you prefer. Just be aware that your animals could turn out smaller or larger depending on the hook size you use.

SAFETY EYES

Safety eyes come in a wide variety of sizes and colors. They have a plastic or metal washer that attaches to the back of the eye once inserted into the crocheted piece. Make sure you have positioned the eyes exactly where you would like before attaching the backs, as they are impossible to remove once attached. Buttons, felt, or embroidered eyes are a great alternative to safety eyes.

For the patterns in this book, we will be using solid black eyes in the following sizes: 9mm, 10mm, 10.5mm, and 12mm. If you plan on giving the items you make to small children, I always recommend replacing the safety eyes with felt or embroidering them on with yarn or embroidery floss.

FIBERFILL STUFFING

Polyester fiberfill is great for stuffing amigurumi. Make sure to add enough so that the piece will hold its shape, but be sure to not overstuff. Adding too much will cause the stitches to stretch and the fiberfill to show through. Use a chopstick or the end of a crochet hook to help get fiberfill into smaller parts that your fingers can't reach.

YARN NEEDLE

An essential part of amigurumi! Also called a darning or tapestry needle, yarn needles are ideal for sewing pieces together or weaving in ends. They have a blunt tip and a much larger eye, making it super easy to thread yarn onto it.

STITCH MARKERS

Stitch markers are a must when making amigurumi! Because we will be crocheting in the round, we'll need to use one of these to mark the end of the previous round. Alternatively, you can use a contrasting piece of yarn or a safety pin instead.

EMBROIDERY NEEDLE AND FLOSS

These are used for adding the finer details to amigurumi, like mouths and noses. I like to use embroidery floss when adding these details because it comes in so many different colors and is a lot thinner than yarn. For the projects in this book, we'll be using black, dark green, and pink embroidery floss.

SCISSORS

A sharp pair of scissors will come in handy for cutting out felt shapes or trimming yarn and embroidery floss.

STRAIGHT PINS

Before assembling the pieces of your animal, use straight pins to position the items. This will help you make sure your items are right where you want them before you commit to sewing them on.

FELT

I love using felt to add small details and texture to an animal. Things like noses and eyes can be easily made using different colored felt. Use a hot glue gun or embroidery floss to attach the felt to the crocheted pieces. For these projects, we'll be using black, pink, and lime green felt.

ALUMINUM CRAFT WIRE

Much thicker and sturdier than pipe cleaners, craft wire is helpful in making larger pieces bend. We'll be using 16 gauge aluminum craft wire for the Snake pattern found in the Jungle chapter (page 88).

HOT GLUE GUN

I love using a hot glue gun to attach felt or crocheted details to a piece. The outcome is always much cleaner and gives the animal a polished look. The trick is to go slow and only add a little bit of glue at a time. Gluing these kinds of details in place is much faster than sewing. If you prefer to not use hot glue, sewing with embroidery floss and a needle is a great alternative.

PET SLICKER BRUSH

One of my favorite tools to use! Using a pet slicker brush helps fluff up the yarn and give the piece a different texture. Use this brush on the tail of the Squirrel (page 164).

ABBREVIATIONS

All patterns in this book are written using U.S. crochet terminology.

BLO - Back Loops Only

Bo - Bobble

Ch - Chain

Dc - Double Crochet

Dc Inc - Double Crochet Increase

Dec - Decrease

FLO - Front Loops Only

Hdc - Half Double Crochet

Hdc Inc - Half Double Crochet Increase

Inc - Increase

Inv Dec - Invisible Decrease

Mini Bo - Mini Bobble

Mr - Magic Ring

R- Round or Row

Sc - Single Crochet

Sl St - Slip Stitch

St/s - Stitch/es

Tr - Treble Crochet

Tr Inc - Treble Crochet Increase

Yo - Yarn Over

* - Repeat the steps between asterisks as many times as stated.
( ) - The number inside the parentheses will indicate how many stitches you will have at the end of the round or row.

STITCHES AND TECHNIQUES

For extra help, video tutorials on how to do these stitches can be found on my blog, www.amenagerieofstitchesblog.com, and on my YouTube channel, A Menagerie of Stitches.

GAUGE
While gauge is an important step in crocheting, for amigurumi it isn't too important. Everyone holds the yarn differently, so your tension may be different than mine. Make sure your tension is even throughout and that your stitches aren't too loose, allowing the fiberfill to show through. Keep in mind that using a smaller or larger hook size and different yarn will change the size of your toys. Measurements for each project are given and are a rough estimate of what the finished sizes will be.

YARN OVER (YO)
To yarn over, simply take your hook and grab hold of the yarn. The yarn will go from the back to the front of the hook. (photo 1) The yarn will be going over your hook, and then you can proceed to pull it through the loop or stitch.

MAGIC RING (MR)

To make a magic ring:
1. Make a loop and place the working yarn on top of the loose tail. (photo 1)
2. Insert hook into loop, grabbing the working yarn with the hook. Pull through the loop. (photos 2+3)
3. Yarn over and pull hook through loop. This is considered a "Ch 1." (photos 4+5)
   This next step is where you will start making single crochets into the magic ring.
4. Insert the hook back into the loop, making sure to go underneath both loops. (photo 6)
5. Yarn over and pull hook through loop. 2 loops will be on the hook. (photos 7+8)

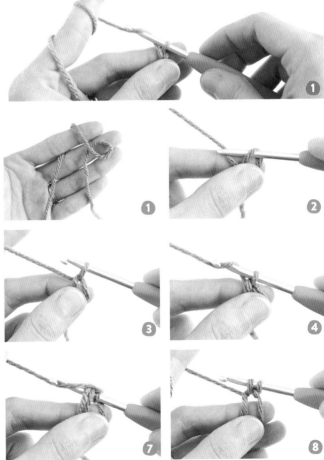

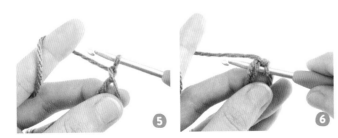

6. Yarn over and pull through both loops. 1 loop will remain on the hook. This completes your first single crochet. (photo 9)
7. Repeat steps 4-6 as many times as pattern states. Most patterns state to do six single crochets in a magic ring. (photo 10)
8. Finally, grab the loose tail and pull to close the loop. You now have a completed magic ring. (photo 11)

To begin the next round, place the next stitch into the first single crochet made in step 6. (photo 12)

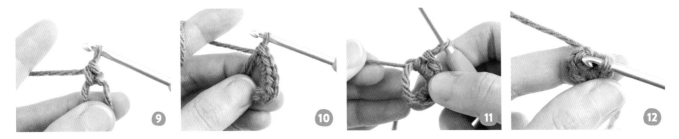

SINGLE CROCHET (SC)
1. Insert hook into stitch and yarn over. (photos 1+2)
2. Pull hook through stitch. There will be 2 loops on your hook. (photo 3)
3. Yarn over again and pull through both loops. 1 loop will remain on hook. (photos 4+5)

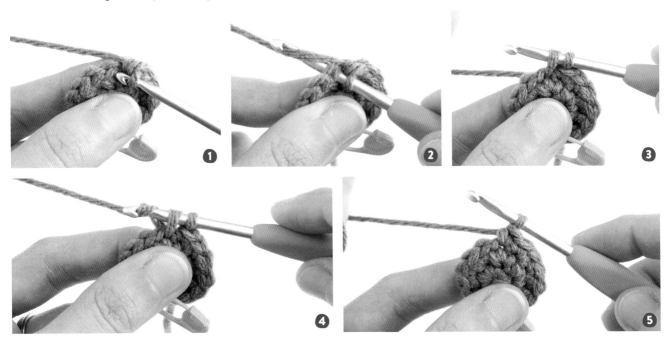

INCREASE (INC)

An increase is used to expand your piece and make it bigger. To increase, simply place 2 single crochets into 1 stitch. If you look at the photo, you'll see 2 "Vs" in one stitch. (photo 1) This is an increase.

HALF DOUBLE CROCHET (HDC)

1. Yarn over and insert hook into stitch. (photos 1+2)
2. Yarn over and pull hook through stitch. 3 loops will remain on the hook. (photos 3+4)
3. Yarn over and pull through all 3 loops. 1 loop will remain on the hook. (photos 5+6)

DOUBLE CROCHET (DC)

1. Yarn over and insert hook into stitch. (photos 1+2)
2. Yarn over and pull hook through stitch. 3 loops will remain on the hook. (photos 3+4)
3. Yarn over and pull through 2 loops only. 2 loops will remain on the hook. (photos 5+6)
4. Yarn over for a final time and pull hook through remaining 2 loops. 1 loop will remain on the hook. (photos 7+8)

12

TREBLE CROCHET (TR)

1. Yarn over 2 times so that 3 loops are on the hook. (photo 1)
2. Insert hook into stitch and yarn over. (photo 2)
3. Pull hook through stitch. There will be 4 loops on your hook. (photo 3)
4. Yarn over and pull through 2 loops. 3 loops will remain on the hook. (photos 4+5)
5. Yarn over again and pull through another 2 loops. 2 loops will remain on the hook. (photos 6+7)
6. Yarn over for a final time and pull through the remaining 2 loops. 1 loop will remain on the hook. (photo 8)

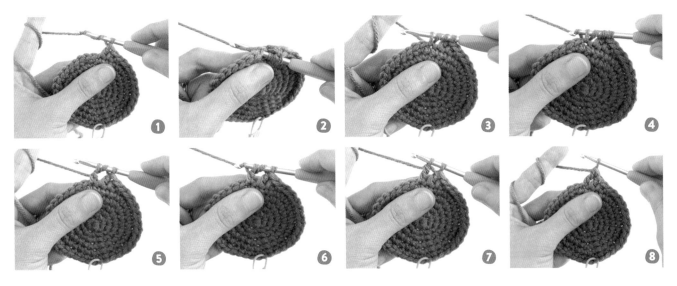

HALF DOUBLE CROCHET, DOUBLE CROCHET, TREBLE CROCHET INCREASE (HDC INC, DC INC, TR INC)

These are just like the regular single crochet increase. Simply place 2 half double crochet stitches, 2 double crochet stitches, or 2 treble crochet stitches into one stitch to create the increase.

INVISIBLE DECREASE (INV DEC)

This is my favorite way to decrease amigurumi. A normal decrease tends to add a little bulk to the finished piece, whereas an invisible decrease is nearly impossible to spot.

To invisible decrease:
1. Insert the hook into the FRONT loops only of the next 2 stitches. There will be 3 loops on your hook. (photo 1)
2. Yarn over and pull hook through the 2 front loops. 2 loops will remain on the hook. (photos 2+3)
3. Yarn over again and pull through the 2 remaining loops. 1 loop will remain on the hook. (photo 4)

REGULAR DECREASE (DEC)

A couple patterns use this technique for decreasing, which is mainly used when working flat pieces and not in the round.

To make a regular decrease:
1. Insert the hook into the next stitch. Yarn over and pull hook through. There will be 2 loops on the hook. (photos 1+2)
2. Insert the hook into the next stitch. Yarn over and pull hook through. There will be 3 loops on the hook. (photos 3-5)
3. Yarn over for the last time and pull through all 3 loops. 1 loop will remain on the hook. (photos 6+7)

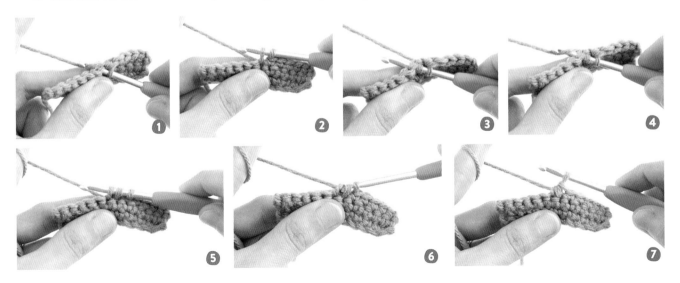

SLIP KNOT

1. Make a loop and place the loose tail on top of the working yarn. (photo 1)
2. Insert hook into loop and grab the loose tail. (photos 2+3)
3. Pull the loose tail through the loop. (photo 4)
4. Holding both tails, pull to tighten the slip knot onto the hook. (photo 5)

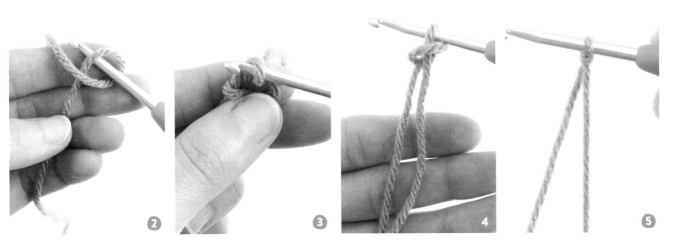

CHAIN (CH)

1. After you have made a slip knot, simply take the working yarn and yarn over. (photo 1)
2. Pull hook through the slip knot. This is your first chain stitch. Repeat as many times as the pattern states. (photos 2+3)

SLIP STITCH (SL ST)

1. Insert hook into stitch or chain and yarn over. (photos 1-3)
2. Pull hook through the stitch or chain. There will be 2 loops on your hook. (photo 4)
3. Pull hook through the first loop. 1 loop will remain on hook. (photos 5+6)

FRONT OR BACK LOOPS ONLY (FLO OR BLO)

Some of the patterns in this book use this technique. When holding your work, you'll see from the top that the stitches look like a sideways "V". The side closest to you is the front loop (photo 1), and the one behind is the back loop. (photo 2) When the pattern states to crochet "In FLO", work the stitches in the front loops only. (photo 3) After crocheting a few stitches, you'll notice the back loops are visible since we aren't working in them. (photo 4) When the pattern states to crochet "In BLO", insert hook into the center of the V, going under the back loop. (photo 5) Again, after a few stitches made in the back loops, you'll notice the front loops are visible. (photo 6)

16

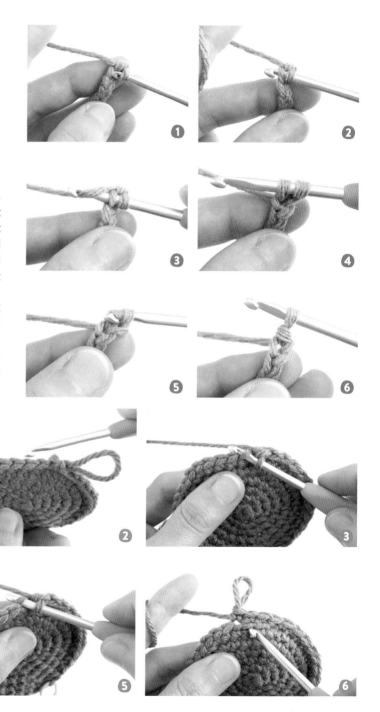

BOBBLE STITCH (BO)

1. Yarn over and insert hook into stitch. (photos 1+2)
2. Yarn over and pull hook through the same stitch. There will be 3 loops on your hook. (photo 3)
3. Yarn over and pull through the first 2 loops. 2 loops will remain on your hook. (photos 4+5)
4. Repeat steps 1-3 a total of 4 more times until there are 6 loops on your hook. (photo 6)
5. Yarn over and pull through all loops on hook. 1 loop will remain on your hook. (photos 7+8)

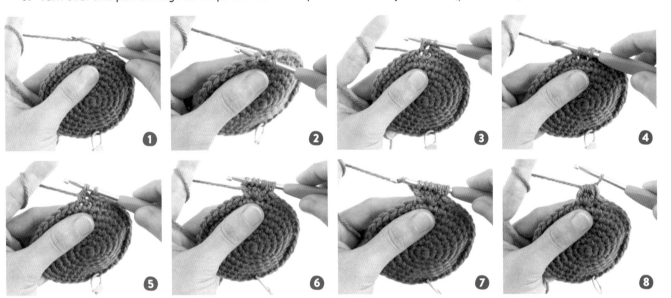

MINI BOBBLE (MINI BO)

1. Yarn over and insert hook into stitch. (photos 1+2)
2. Yarn over and pull hook through the same stitch. There will be 3 loops on your hook. (photo 3)
3. Yarn over and pull through the first 2 loops. 2 loops will remain on your hook. (photos 4+5)
4. Repeat steps 1 and 2 once more until there are 3 loops on your hook. (photo 6)
5. Yarn over and pull through all loops on hook. 1 loop will remain on your hook. (photos 7+8)

CLEAN COLOR CHANGE

A clean color change is used when you don't want the color change to be as noticeable. While the color change is still visible, it's a lot less drastic.

1. When working the last stitch of the old color, single crochet until there are just 2 loops left on the hook. (photo 1)
2. Use the new color to yarn over and complete the stitch. (photos 2+3)
3. Slip stitch into the next stitch with the new color. (photos 4-6)
4. Continue to crochet as normal with the new color. (photo 7)

Trim the tail of the old color. Tie the tails from both colors together to secure the color change. I used this method on the stripes of the clownfish.

REGULAR COLOR CHANGE

A regular color change is great if you want the color change to be more visible. By doing this method, the stitch in the new color is more noticeable than if you were to use the "Clean Color Change" method.

Use this method on the toucan's beak (page 106) and the fox's legs and tail (page 120).

1. When working the last stitch of the old color, single crochet until there are just 2 loops left on the hook. (photo 1)

18

2. Use the new color to yarn over and complete the stitch. (photos 2+3)
3. Single crochet into the next stitch and continue crocheting as normal with the new color. (photos 4+5)

Trim the tail of the old color. Tie the tails from both colors together to secure the color change.

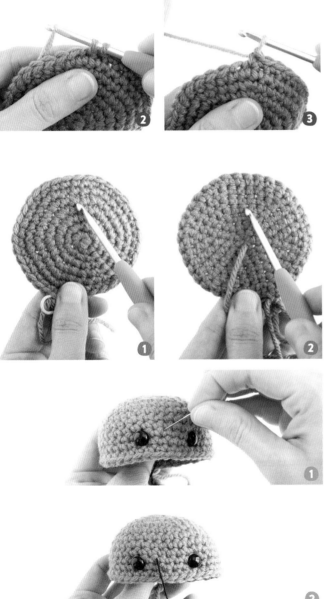

RIGHT SIDE/WRONG SIDE OF WORK

When working your pieces, you'll notice that one side will always be facing you. This side is considered the "right" side of the work. The side facing away from you is the "wrong" side, or the back side of the work. One way to decipher which side is which is to simply look at the side facing you and look for the "V". (photo 1) If you turn your work over to the back side, you'll notice that there is a horizontal bar in between each row of "V's". (photo 2) Sometimes the work tends to curl in the opposite direction, which causes the "wrong" side of the work to end up on the outside of the finished piece. If it does curl, just make sure to correct it so the "right" side is always facing you.

ADDING A MOUTH

Thread your embroidery needle with a length of embroidery floss about 5-6 inches long.
1. Bring the needle from inside the piece to the outside, near the safety eye on your left. (photos 1+2)
2. Go across to the right side and insert the needle into the piece. Pull the needle through but make sure to not pull the floss all the way through. (photo 3)
3. Hold the thread in a smile shape and bring the needle through to the outside of the piece. You'll want to come out about one round down and in the center from where we first inserted the needle in step 1. (photos 4+5)

4. Pull the thread down to make a "V" shape. (photo 6)
5. Insert the needle very close to the spot where it just came out. You'll bring the needle around the main piece of floss making the smile and then insert it back into the piece. (photo 7)
6. Pull the thread through and make a knot to secure floss. (photo 8)

CLOSING UP YOUR PIECE

I like using this closing technique because it gives the piece a more finished look and the closure is nearly invisible.

1. When you've reached the end of the piece, cut the yarn and leave a tail for closing. Pull the yarn tail all the way through and pull to secure. (photos 1+2)
2. Thread the yarn tail onto the needle. Insert the needle into the front loop of the first stitch, working from the center to the outside. Pull the needle through. Continue going through the front loops of the remaining stitches. (photo 3)
3. Once you have reached the end, pull the yarn tail and the hole will close. (photos 4+5)
4. Insert the needle into the center of the hole and bring out on the side of the piece. Secure with a knot, trim tail and hide inside piece. (photos 6-8)

CLEAN FASTEN OFF

This is my favorite way to fasten off, as it gives you a clean edge and makes attaching the pieces much easier.

1. Once you reach the last stitch, cut the yarn and then pull the loop that was just on the hook all the way until the tail comes through. (photos 1-3)

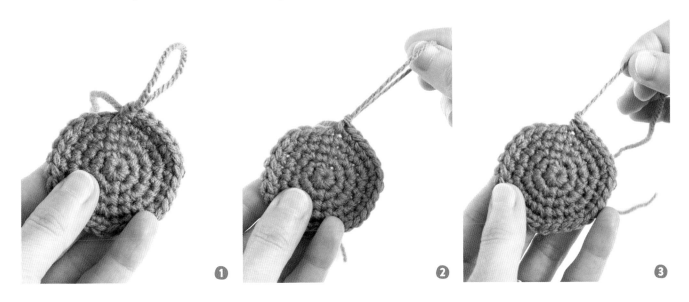

2. With a yarn needle, skip the first stitch of the round, the one directly next to our last stitch of the round, and go to the 2nd stitch.
3. Going from front to back, weave the needle under both loops (the "V"). Pull the yarn through. (photos 4+5)
4. Then weave the needle in between the "V" of the last stitch of the round, going from the front to the back. Only go under the back loop for this. (photo 6)
5. Pull the yarn through, making sure to not pull too tight. You'll notice that we just created a "stitch" and the fasten off is invisible. (photos 7-9)

Either weave in the tail or leave it for sewing, whichever the pattern states.

CROCHET TIPS

SKILL LEVELS

At the beginning of each pattern, you'll find the project skill level, which is indicated by a pair of scissors. One pair of scissors represents a beginner-friendly project, two pairs indicates an intermediate project, and three pairs indicates an expert project.

For beginners, I recommend flipping through the book and finding some of the easier projects to get started. If you have experience with crochet and are looking for more of a challenge, try out the expert patterns.

TIPS FOR READING A PATTERN

Most, if not all, of these patterns are crocheted in the round, or a continuous spiral. Do not join and chain after each round. Use a stitch marker to mark the last stitch in the round, moving it up as you complete each round.

When the number comes **AFTER** the stitch, such as *Sc 3*, this means to place one single crochet into the next three stitches.

Example: *Sc 3, inc* 6 times. (30 sts)

You would make one single crochet into the next 3 stitches, then increase (inc) by placing 2 single crochets together into the next stitch. You will repeat this sequence 6 times and will end with 30 stitches in that round.

When the number comes **BEFORE** the stitch, such as *3 Sc*, this means to place three single crochet stitches into the same stitch.

If you see, for example, "**R8-11**: Sc 36" this means you will continue crocheting 36 stitches total for rounds 8, 9, 10, and 11. I like to have a piece of paper and a pencil handy for keeping track of my rounds.

If there are two or more stitches listed in between commas, such as "Sc, **hdc dc**, sc", this means to place both an hdc and dc together in one stitch.

OCEAN

CLOWNFISH

EXPERT

FINISHED MEASUREMENTS

- ✗ Approx. 3 inches wide by 3.5 inches tall by 7.5 inches long

MATERIALS

- ✗ Worsted weight yarn: Orange, Black, and White
- ✗ Size F/3.75mm crochet hook
- ✗ One pair of 9mm safety eyes
- ✗ Polyester fiberfill stuffing
- ✗ Yarn needle
- ✗ Scissors
- ✗ Stitch marker
- ✗ Straight pins

ABBREVIATIONS

- ✗ Ch- Chain
- ✗ Dc- Double Crochet
- ✗ Dec- Decrease
- ✗ Hdc- Half Double Crochet
- ✗ Inc- Increase
- ✗ Inv Dec- Invisible Decrease
- ✗ R- Round/Row
- ✗ Sc- Single Crochet
- ✗ St/s- Stitch/es

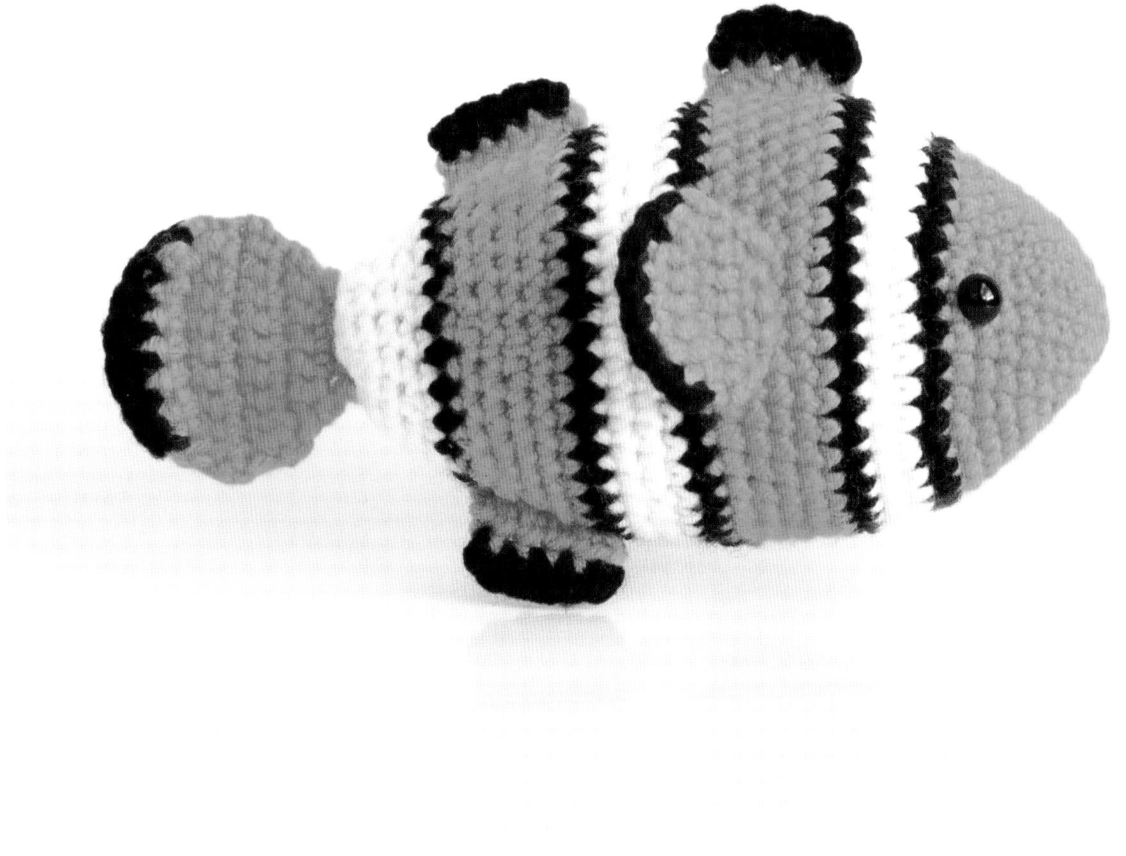

BODY

Note: There are quite a few color changes for this part of the pattern. When changing colors, simply drop the old color, pick up the new color, and continue crocheting as normal. This pattern is written so that when there is a color change, all you have to do is carry the yarn up the couple of rounds where it was last dropped.

Using orange yarn,

R1	6 sc in magic ring. (6 sts)
R2	Inc in each st around. (12 sts)
R3	*Sc 1, inc* 6 times. (18 sts)
R4	Sc 18.
R5	*Sc 2, inc* 6 times. (24 sts)
R6	Sc 24.
R7	*Sc 3, inc* 6 times. (30 sts)
R8	Sc 30.
R9	*Sc 4, inc* 6 times. (36 sts)

Change to black yarn,

R10	Sc 36.

Change to white yarn,

R11	*Sc 5, inc* 6 times. (42 sts)
R12	Sc 42.

Add the safety eyes between rounds 8 and 9, placing them 13 stitches apart. (photo 1)

Change to black yarn,

R13	Sc 42.

Change to orange yarn,

R14-18	Sc 42.

Change to black yarn,

R19	Sc 42.

Change to white yarn,

R20-22	Sc 42.

Change to black yarn,

R23	Sc 42.

Change to orange yarn,

R24+25	Sc 42.
R26	*Sc 5, inv dec* 6 times. (36 sts)
R27	Sc 36.
R28	*Sc 4, inv dec* 6 times. (30 sts)

Begin adding fiberfill and continue adding as you close the piece.

Change to black yarn,

R29	*Sc 3, inv dec* 6 times. (24 sts)

Fasten off black and orange yarn.

Change to white yarn,

R30	Sc 24.
R31	*Sc 2, inv dec* 6 times. (18 sts)
R32+33	Sc 18.
R34	*Sc 1, inv dec* 6 times. (12 sts)
R35	Inv dec around 6 times. (6 sts)

Fasten off and leave a tail to close the piece. (photos 2+3)

SIDE FINS: MAKE 2

Using orange yarn,
Leave about 10 inches at the beginning for sewing.

R1   Ch 5 then starting in the 2nd ch from hook and in both loops leaving the back "bump", sc in each chain across. (4 sts) Ch 1 and turn. (photos 4+5)

R2   Inc, sc 2, inc. (6 sts) Ch 1 and turn.

R3   Inc, sc 4, inc. (8 sts) Ch 1 and turn.

R4   Sc 8. Ch 1 and turn.

R5   Dec, sc 4, dec. (6 sts) Ch 1 and turn.

R6   Dec, sc 2, dec. (4 sts)

Fasten off the orange yarn. (photo 6)

R7   Join black yarn on the right side of the fin, in the 2nd hole along the edge, with a ch 1. (photos 7-10) Then sc in the next hole along the edge. (photos 11+12) Next sc across the 4 stitches from R6. (photo 13) Sc in the 1st hole on the edge of the left side. Then sc in the next hole along the edge. (6 sts) (photos 14+15)

Fasten off and weave in all ends except the long tail left at the start. (photos 16+17)

Using straight pins, pin the fins near round 16 on both sides of the body. (photos 18+19) With the yarn needle and the tail left at the beginning, sew the fins to the body. Secure with a knot and hide inside the body. (photos 20+21)

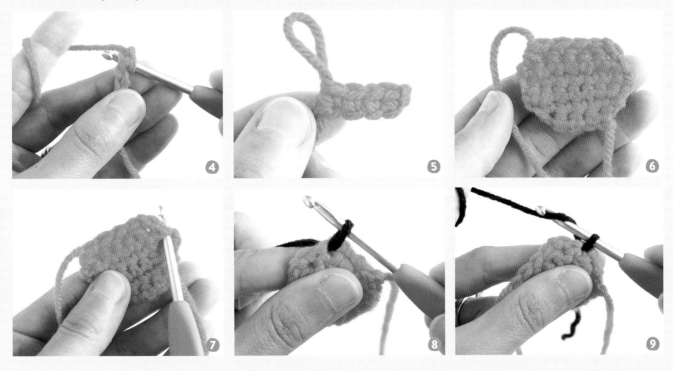

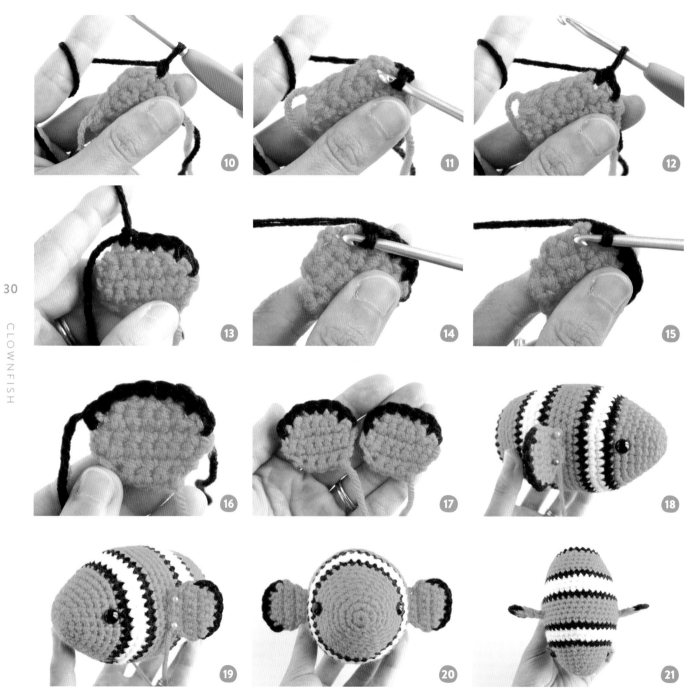

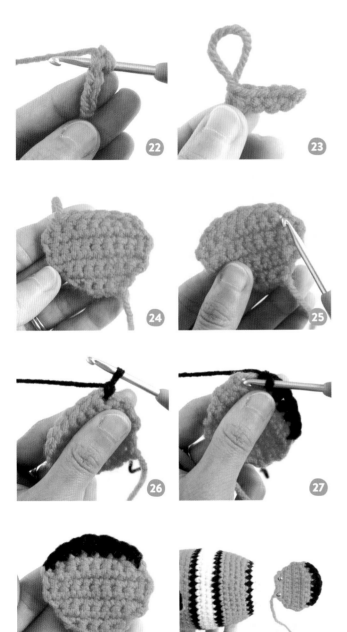

TAIL

Using orange yarn,

Leave about 10 inches at the beginning for sewing.

R1   Ch 5 then starting in the 2nd ch from hook and in both loops leaving the back "bump", sc in each chain across. (4 sts) Ch 1 and turn. (photos 22+23)

R2   Inc, sc 2, inc. (6 sts) Ch 1 and turn.

R3   Inc, sc 4, inc. (8 sts) Ch 1 and turn.

R4   Inc, sc 6, inc. (10 sts) Ch 1 and turn.

R5+6   Sc 10. Ch 1 and turn.

R7   Dec, sc 6, dec. (8 sts) Ch 1 and turn.

R8   Dec, sc 4, dec. (6 sts)

Fasten off the orange yarn. (photo 24)

R9   Join black yarn on the right side of the fin, in the 1st hole along the edge, with a ch 1. (photos 25+26) Working into the stitches from R8: sc, hdc, dc, dc, hdc, sc. Then sc into the 1st hole along the edge of the left side. (8 sts) (photo 27)

Fasten off and weave in all ends except the long tail left at the start. (photo 28)

Using straight pins, pin the tail in the center of the body near rounds 34 and 35. (photo 29) With the yarn needle and the tail left at the beginning, sew the tail to the body. Secure with a knot and hide inside the body. (photo 30)

DORSAL FINS

LARGE: MAKE 2

Using orange yarn,

Leave about 10 inches at the beginning for sewing.

R1   Ch 6 then starting in the 2nd ch from hook and in both loops leaving the back "bump", hdc in each chain across. **(5 sts)** (photos 31+32)

Fasten off orange yarn.

R2   Join black yarn into the first hdc and ch 1. (photos 33-36) Place 1 hdc into the same space as the ch and then hdc across the remaining 4 stitches. **(5 sts)** (photos 37+38)

Fasten off and weave in all ends except the long tail left at the start. (photo 39)

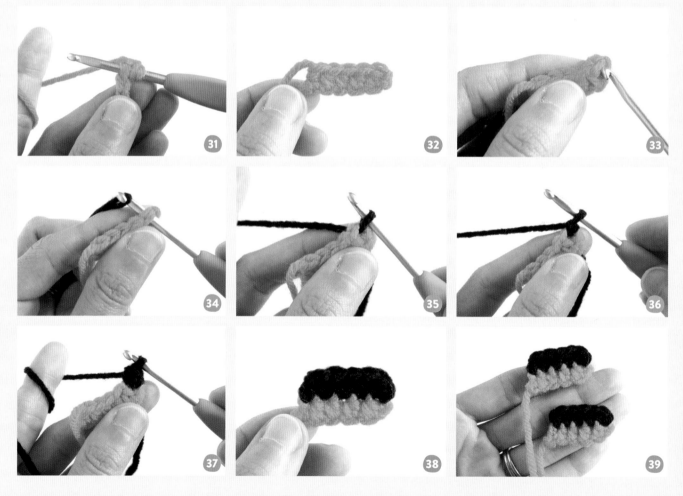

SMALL: MAKE 1

Using orange yarn,

Leave about 10 inches at the beginning for sewing.

R1 Ch 6 then starting in the 2nd ch from hook and in both loops leaving the back "bump", sc in each chain across. (5 sts) (photos 40+41)

Fasten off orange yarn.

R2 Join black yarn into the first sc and ch 1. (photos 42-44) Place 1 sc into the same space as the ch and then sc across the remaining 4 stitches. (5 sts) (photo 45)

Fasten off and weave in all ends except the long tail left at the start. (photo 46)

Using straight pins, pin the fins on the body. Place one large fin between rounds 13-19 on the top of the body. Then place the second large fin on the underside of the body between rounds 23-28. For the small fin, place between rounds 23-28 on the top of the body. Refer to photo 47 for positioning. With the yarn needle and leftover yarn tails from the start, sew the fins into place. Secure with a knot and hide inside the body. (photos 47-50)

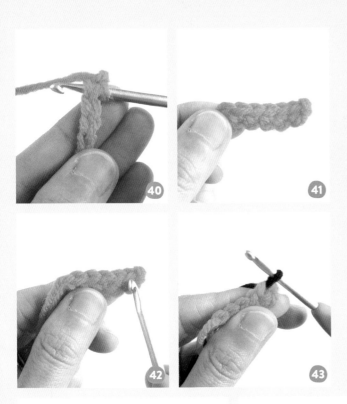

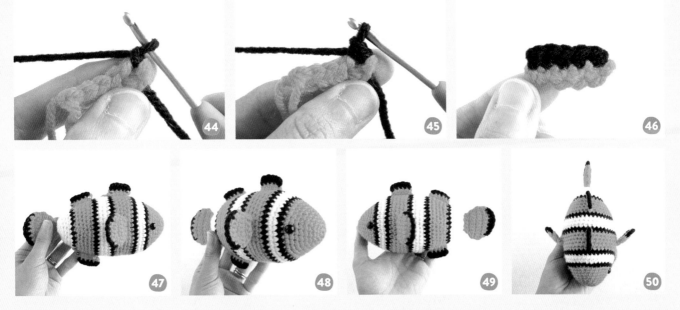

CRAB

INTERMEDIATE

 FINISHED MEASUREMENTS
- Approx. 9 inches wide by 3.5 inches tall

 MATERIALS
- Worsted weight yarn: Red, Light Red, and Peach
- Size F/3.75mm crochet hook
- One pair of 10mm safety eyes
- Black embroidery floss and needle
- Polyester fiberfill stuffing
- Yarn needle
- Scissors
- Stitch marker
- Straight pins

 ABBREVIATIONS
- FLO- Front Loops Only
- Inc- Increase
- Inv Dec- Invisible Decrease
- R- Round
- Sc- Single Crochet
- St/s- Stitch/es

SHELL

Using red yarn,

R1	6 sc in magic ring. (6 sts)
R2	Inc in each st around. (12 sts)
R3	*Sc 1, inc* 6 times. (18 sts)
R4	*Sc 2, inc* 6 times. (24 sts)
R5	*Sc 3, inc* 6 times. (30 sts)
R6	*Sc 4, inc* 6 times. (36 sts)
R7	*Sc 5, inc* 6 times. (42 sts)
R8	*Sc 6, inc* 6 times. (48 sts)
R9-16	Sc 48.

Add safety eyes between rounds 12 and 13, placing them 5 stitches apart. Using black embroidery floss, sew on the mouth. (photo 1)

R17	In FLO, Sc 48. (photo 2)
R18	Sc 48.

Fasten off and weave in the end. (photo 3)

Using light red yarn, make the speckles on the shell. Starting near round 5, make eight lines in a cluster. Make a cluster on each side of the shell and above the eyes. (photos 4+5)

BELLY

Using peach yarn,

R1	6 sc in magic ring. (6 sts)
R2	Inc in each st around. (12 sts)
R3	*Sc 1, inc* 6 times. (18 sts)
R4	*Sc 2, inc* 6 times. (24 sts)
R5	*Sc 3, inc* 6 times. (30 sts)
R6	*Sc 4, inc* 6 times. (36 sts)
R7	*Sc 5, inc* 6 times. (42 sts)
R8	*Sc 6, inc* 6 times. (48 sts)

Fasten off and leave a long tail for sewing. (photo 6)

With the yarn needle, sew the belly to the shell. Weave the needle under the back loops left over from R17 of the shell and then under both loops (the "V") from the stitches on R8 of the body. (photos 7+8)

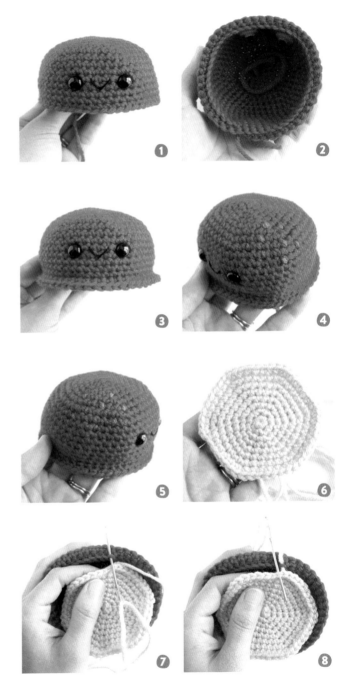

Then go over to the next stitch and repeat. (photo 9) Make sure to go under the stitches and not over them to create a clean finish on the belly. (photos 10+11) Add fiberfill to the shell before closing the piece. (photo 12) Once you reach the end, secure with a knot and hide inside the shell. (photos 13+14)

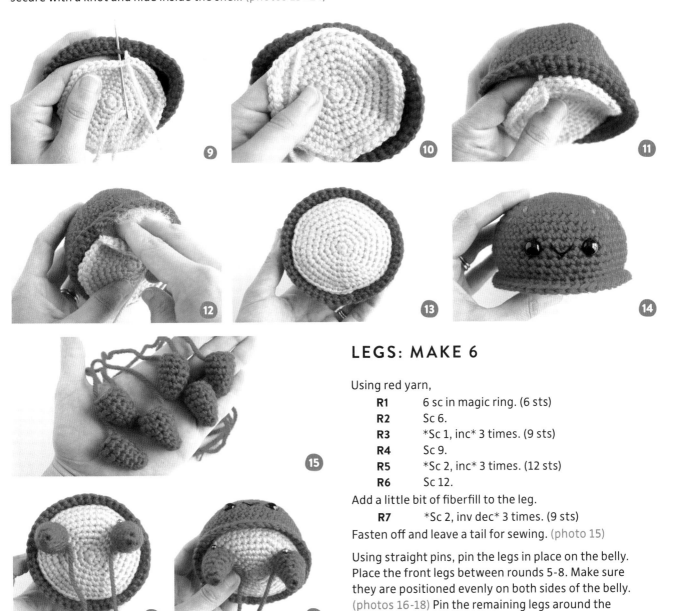

LEGS: MAKE 6

Using red yarn,

R1	6 sc in magic ring. (6 sts)
R2	Sc 6.
R3	*Sc 1, inc* 3 times. (9 sts)
R4	Sc 9.
R5	*Sc 2, inc* 3 times. (12 sts)
R6	Sc 12.

Add a little bit of fiberfill to the leg.

R7	*Sc 2, inv dec* 3 times. (9 sts)

Fasten off and leave a tail for sewing. (photo 15)

Using straight pins, pin the legs in place on the belly. Place the front legs between rounds 5-8. Make sure they are positioned evenly on both sides of the belly. (photos 16-18) Pin the remaining legs around the belly, curving them slightly so they form a "V" shape.

The back legs will be closer together. (photo 19) Then, with the yarn needle and the tail, sew the legs to the belly. Secure with a knot and hide inside the shell. (photos 20+21)

CLAWS

The claws are worked in two pieces. First, crochet the smaller piece and then join where indicated in the pattern for the bigger piece.

SMALL PIECE: MAKE 2

Using red yarn,

R1	6 sc in magic ring. (6 sts)
R2	Sc 6.
R3	*Sc 1, inc* 3 times. (9 sts)

Fasten off and leave a small tail for sewing. (photo 22) Set aside.

BIG PIECE: MAKE 2

Using red yarn,

R1	6 sc in magic ring. (6 sts)
R2	Sc 6.
R3	*Sc 1, inc* 3 times. (9 sts)
R4	Sc 9.
R5	*Sc 2, inc* 3 times. (12 sts)
R6	Sc 12.
R7	*Sc 3, inc* 3 times. (15 sts) (photo 23)

We're now going to connect the small piece to the big piece and then will continue with the rest of the claw. (photo 24)

| R8 | With the big piece still on the hook, insert the hook into the first stitch on the small piece and sc. This will be the stitch to the left of where we fastened off. (photo 25) Sc 9 times total on the small piece. Then, on the big piece, you'll insert the hook into the first stitch we |

made in R7. (photo 26) Sc 15 times total on the big piece. (24 sts) (photo 27)

| R9 | *Sc 4, inv dec* 4 times. (20 sts) (photo 28) |
| R10 | *Sc 8, inv dec* 2 times. (18 sts) (photo 29) |

Use the yarn needle and the tail left over from the small piece to sew the opening between the pieces closed. (photo 30) Secure with a knot inside the claw.

Add fiberfill to the tips of both pieces and continue adding as you work the piece.

R11	Sc 18.
R12	*Sc 1, inv dec* 6 times. (12 sts) (photo 31)
R13	*Sc 2, inv dec* 3 times. (9 sts)
R14-18	Sc 9. (photo 32)

Fasten off and leave a tail for sewing. (photo 33)

Using straight pins, pin the claws to the shell between rounds 14-16. (photo 34) With the yarn needle and the tail, sew the claws to the shell. Secure with a knot and hide inside the shell. (photos 35+36)

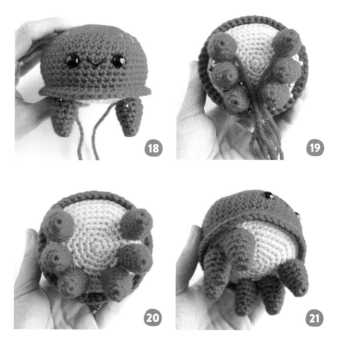

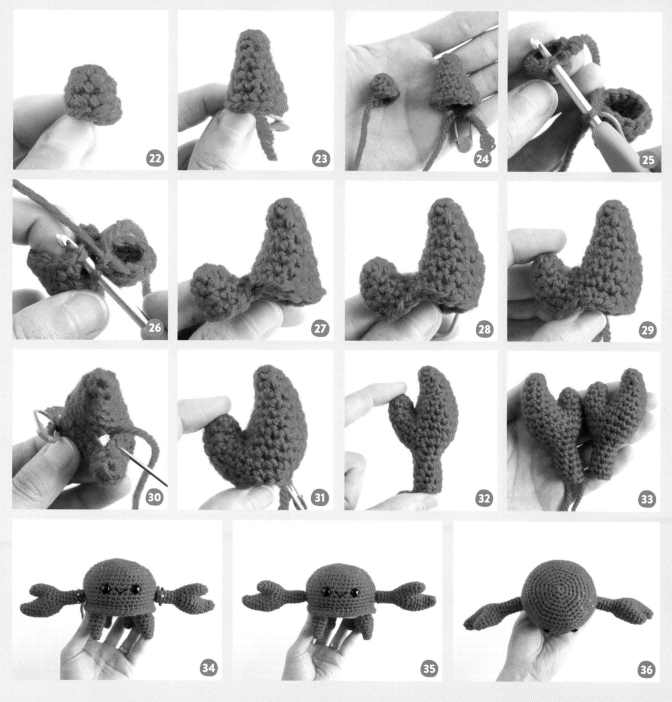

GREAT WHITE SHARK

BEGINNER

 FINISHED MEASUREMENTS
- ✕ Approx. 3 inches wide by 5.5 inches tall by 10 inches long

 MATERIALS
- ✕ Worsted weight yarn: Gray and White
- ✕ Size F/3.75mm crochet hook
- ✕ One pair of 10mm safety eyes
- ✕ Black embroidery floss and needle
- ✕ Polyester fiberfill stuffing
- ✕ Yarn needle
- ✕ Scissors
- ✕ Stitch marker
- ✕ Straight pins

 ABBREVIATIONS
- ✕ Ch- Chain
- ✕ Dec- Decrease
- ✕ Inc- Increase
- ✕ Inv Dec- Invisible Decrease
- ✕ R- Round/Row
- ✕ Sc- Single Crochet
- ✕ St/s- Stitch/es

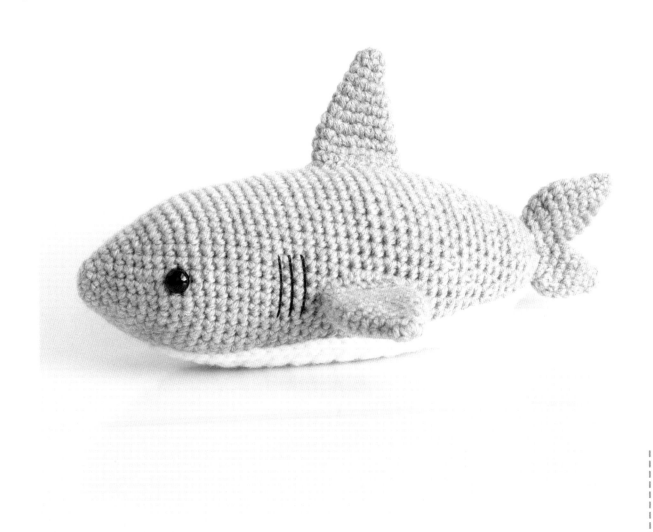

BODY

Using gray yarn,

R1	6 sc in magic ring. (6 sts)
R2	Inc in each st around. (12 sts)
R3	Sc 12.
R4	*Sc 1, inc* 6 times. (18 sts)
R5	Sc 18.
R6	*Sc 2, inc* 6 times. (24 sts)
R7	Sc 24.
R8	*Sc 3, inc* 6 times. (30 sts)
R9	Sc 30.
R10	*Sc 4, inc* 6 times. (36 sts)
R11	Sc 36.
R12	*Sc 5, inc* 6 times. (42 sts)
R13-35	Sc 42.

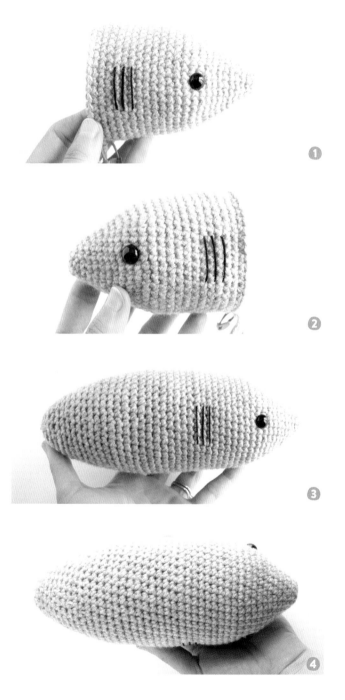

After round 25, add safety eyes and gills. Add the eyes between rounds 11 and 12, placing them 16 stitches apart. For the gills, use black embroidery floss, sew three lines vertically, about 5 stitches long. Stitch these between rounds 20-22. (photos 1+2)

Begin adding fiberfill and continue adding as you close the piece.

R36	*Sc 5, inv dec* 6 times. (36 sts)
R37	Sc 36.
R38	*Sc 4, inv dec* 6 times. (30 sts)
R39+40	Sc 30.
R41	*Sc 3, inv dec* 6 times. (24 sts)
R42+43	Sc 24.
R44	*Sc 2, inv dec* 6 times. (18 sts)
R45	Sc 18.
R46	*Sc 1, inv dec* 6 times. (12 sts)
R47	Sc 12.
R48	Inv dec around 6 times. (6 sts)

Fasten off and leave a tail to close the piece.
(photos 3+4)

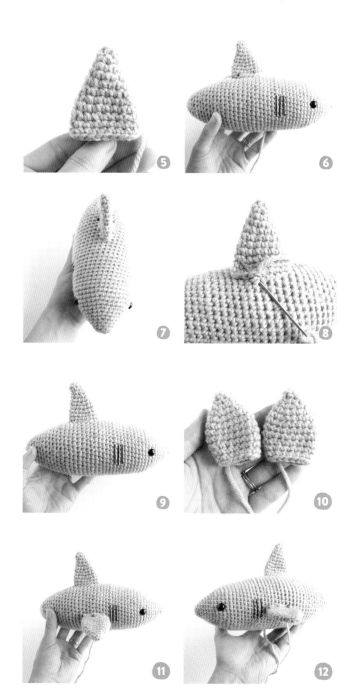

DORSAL FIN

Using gray yarn,

R1	6 sc in magic ring. (6 sts)
R2	Sc 6.
R3	*Sc 1, inc* 3 times. (9 sts)
R4	Sc 9.
R5	*Sc 2, inc* 3 times. (12 sts)
R6	Sc 12.
R7	*Sc 3, inc* 3 times. (15 sts)
R8	Sc 15.
R9	*Sc 4, inc* 3 times. (18 sts)
R10+11	Sc 18.

Fasten off and leave a tail for sewing. Leave fin unstuffed. (photo 5)

Using straight pins, pin the dorsal fin to the body between rounds 26-34. (photos 6+7) With the yarn needle and the tail, sew the fin to the body. (photo 8) Secure with a knot and hide inside the body. (photo 9)

PECTORAL SIDE FINS: MAKE 2

Using gray yarn,

R1	6 sc in magic ring. (6 sts)
R2	Sc 6.
R3	*Sc 1, inc* 3 times. (9 sts)
R4	*Sc 2, inc* 3 times. (12 sts)
R5	*Sc 3, inc* 3 times. (15 sts)
R6	*Sc 4, inc* 3 times. (18 sts)
R7-9	Sc 18.
R10	*Sc 4, inv dec* 3 times. (15 sts)
R11+12	Sc 15.

Fasten off and leave a tail for sewing. Leave fins unstuffed. (photo 10)

Using straight pins, pin the fins to the side of the body between rounds 24-30. (photos 11+12) When positioning them, make sure to line the fins up with the safety eyes. (photos 13+14) With the yarn needle and the tail, sew the fin to the body. Secure with a knot and hide inside the body.

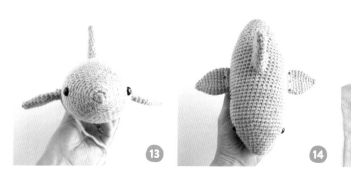

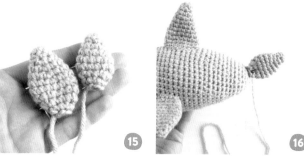

CAUDAL FIN

LARGER TOP PIECE

Using gray yarn,

R1	6 sc in magic ring. (6 sts)
R2	Sc 6.
R3	*Sc 1, inc* 3 times. (9 sts)
R4	*Sc 2, inc* 3 times. (12 sts)
R5	*Sc 3, inc* 3 times. (15 sts)
R6+7	Sc 15.
R8	*Sc 3, inv dec* 3 times. (12 sts)
R9	*Sc 2, inv dec* 3 times. (9 sts)
R10	*Sc 1, inv dec* 3 times. (6 sts)

Fasten off and leave a tail for sewing. Leave fin unstuffed. (photo 15)

SMALLER BOTTOM PIECE

Using gray yarn,

R1	6 sc in magic ring. (6 sts)
R2	Sc 6.
R3	*Sc 1, inc* 3 times. (9 sts)
R4	*Sc 2, inc* 3 times. (12 sts)
R5+6	Sc 12.
R7	*Sc 2, inv dec* 3 times. (9 sts)
R8	*Sc 1, inv dec* 3 times. (6 sts)

Fasten off and leave a tail for sewing. Leave fin unstuffed. (photo 15)

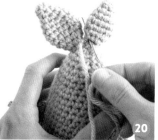

To assemble the tail: pin the larger top piece in place on the tip of the tail near rounds 47 and 48. (photo 16) Make sure this piece lines up with the dorsal fin on top of the body. With the yarn needle and the tail, sew the fin to the body. Next, pin the smaller bottom piece directly under the top piece. (photo 17) Sew into place. Using the same tail, sew the two pieces together about 2-3 rounds from where they connect at the body. (photos 18-21) Secure both with a knot and hide inside the body. (photo 22)

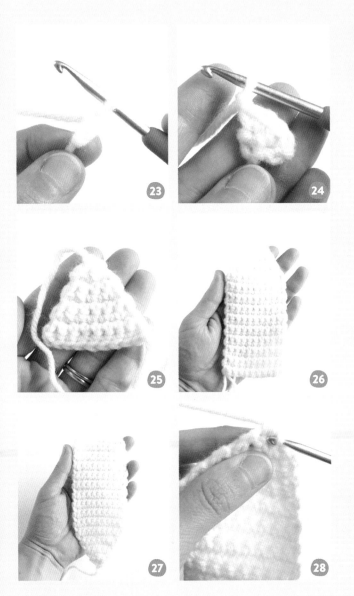

BELLY

Using white yarn,

R1	Ch 2 then in the 2nd ch from hook, inc. (2 sts) Ch 1 and turn. (photo 23)
R2	Inc in each st across. (4 sts) Ch 1 and turn. (photo 24)
R3	Sc 4. Ch 1 and turn.
R4	Inc, sc 2, inc. (6 sts) Ch 1 and turn.
R5	Sc 6. Ch 1 and turn.
R6	Inc, sc 4, inc. (8 sts) Ch 1 and turn.
R7	Sc 8. Ch 1 and turn.
R8	Inc, sc 6, inc. (10 sts) Ch 1 and turn. (photo 25)
R9-27	Sc 10. Ch 1 and turn after each row. (photo 26)
R28	Dec, sc 6, dec. (8 sts) Ch 1 and turn.
R29	Sc 8. Ch 1 and turn.
R30	Dec, sc 4, dec. (6 sts) Ch 1 and turn.
R31	Sc 6. Ch 1 and turn.
R32	Dec, sc 2, dec. (4 sts) Ch 1 and turn.
R33	Sc 4. Ch 1 and turn.
R34	Dec 2 times. (2 sts) (photo 27)

For this next row we are going to work around the edge of the belly.

R35	Sc in the same st as the last sc, then continue single crocheting all the way around the edge. (69 sts) (photos 28+29)

Fasten off and leave an extra-long tail for sewing.

Using the straight pins, pin the belly to the body of the shark, starting near round 10 and ending near round 45. (photos 30+31) With the yarn needle and the tail, weave under both loops (the "V") from the stitches on R35 of the belly and then into the body. (photos 32) Then weave the needle back into the body and under the next stitch on the belly piece. (photo 33) Make sure to go under the stitches and not over them to create a clean finish. Once you reach the end, secure with a knot and hide inside the body. (photos 34-36)

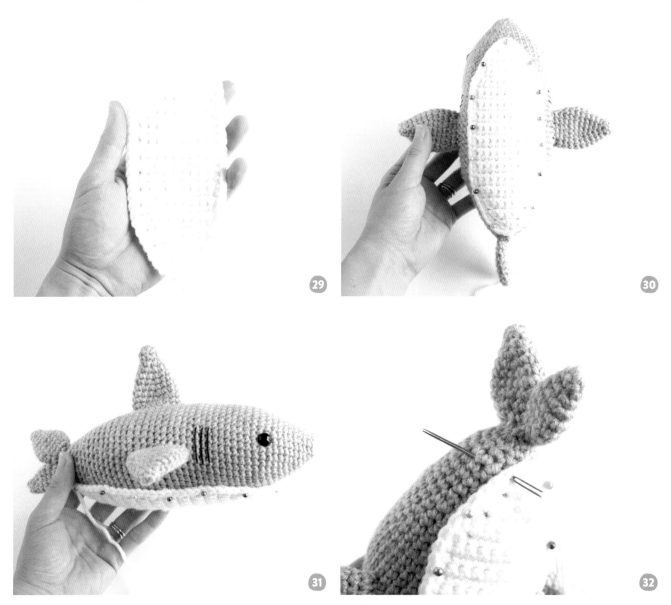

MANTA RAY

BEGINNER

FINISHED MEASUREMENTS
✕ Approx. 6.5 inches wide by 2 inches tall by 7.5 inches long

MATERIALS
✕ Worsted weight yarn: Blue and White
✕ Size F/3.75mm crochet hook
✕ One pair of 9mm safety eyes
✕ Black embroidery floss and needle
✕ Polyester fiberfill stuffing
✕ Yarn needle
✕ Scissors
✕ Stitch marker

ABBREVIATIONS
✕ Ch- Chain
✕ Dec- Decrease
✕ Inc- Increase
✕ R- Round/Row
✕ Sc- Single Crochet
✕ St/s- Stitch/es

BODY: MAKE 2

(ONE BLUE, ONE WHITE)

Using blue or white yarn,

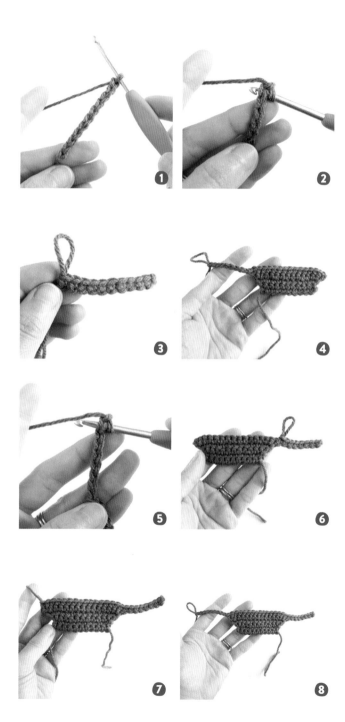

R1 Ch 11 then starting in the 2nd ch from hook and in both loops leaving the back "bump", sc in each chain across. (10 sts) Ch 1 and turn. (photos 1-3)

R2 Sc 10. Ch 1 and turn.

R3 Inc, sc 8, inc. (12 sts) Ch 1 and turn.

R4 Inc, sc 10, inc. (14 sts) Ch 1 and turn.

R5 Inc, sc 12, inc. (16 sts) Ch 9 and turn. (photo 4)

R6 Starting in the 2nd ch from hook and in both loops leaving the back "bump", sc in each chain across (8 times). (photos 5+6) Then, continuing on the main body, sc 16. (24 sts) (photo 7) Ch 9 and turn. (photo 8)

R7 Starting in the 2nd ch from hook and in both loops leaving the back "bump", sc in each chain across (8 times). (photos 9+10) Then, continuing on the main body, sc 24. (32 sts) (photo 11) Ch 1 and turn.

R8+9 Sc 32. Ch 1 and turn. (photo 12)

R10 Dec, sc 28, dec. (30 sts) Ch 1 and turn.

R11 Sc 30. Ch 1 and turn. (photo 13)

R12 Dec, sc 26, dec. (28 sts) Ch 1 and turn.

R13 Dec, sc 24, dec. (26 sts) Ch 1 and turn.

R14 Dec, sc 22, dec. (24 sts) Ch 1 and turn.

R15 Dec, sc 20, dec. (22 sts) Ch 1 and turn. (photo 14)

R16 Dec 2 times, sc 14, dec 2 times. (18 sts) Ch 1 and turn.

R17 Dec 2 times, sc 10, dec 2 times. (14 sts) Ch 1 and turn. (photo 15)

R18 Dec, sc 10, dec. (12 sts) Ch 1 and turn.

R19 Dec, sc 8, dec. (10 sts) Ch 1 and turn.

R20+21 Sc 10. Ch 1 and turn. (photo 16)

R22 Dec, sc 6, dec. (8 sts) Ch 1 and turn.

R23 Dec, sc 4, dec. (6 sts) (photo 17)

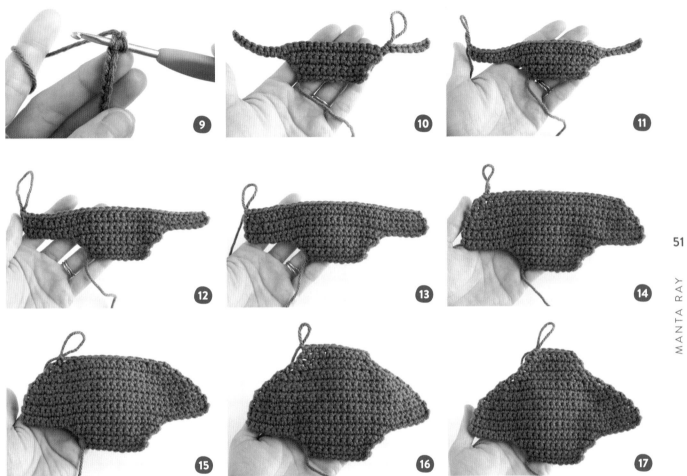

Fasten off on the white piece only. (photo 18) Do not fasten off the blue piece, as we will continue using it to connect the two pieces. On the blue piece, add safety eyes between rows 20 and 21, placing them 4 stitches apart. You should have 2 stitches on the outside of each eye. Sew on mouth. (photo 19)

To assemble: line the two pieces up together. An easy way to do this is to line up where the beginning chain tail is left over. (photo 20) Place a stitch marker through both pieces where the last single crochet was made in R23. (photo 21) This will help keep the two pieces in place while you crochet around. With the blue yarn still on the hook, insert the hook into both pieces along the edge and make a single crochet. (photos 22+23) Continue doing this until you reach the back of the wing. (photos 24+25) When you get to the back of the wing, place the single crochet stitches into the "bumps" that were left over. (photo 26) Do this for the rear of the manta ray, as well as on the opposite wing. (photos 27+28) Pause once you reach the face. (photos 29+30) Add fiberfill to the body only, leaving the wings unstuffed. (photos 31+32) Continue crocheting until you reach the stitch marker. Secure with a knot and hide inside the body. (photos 33-35)

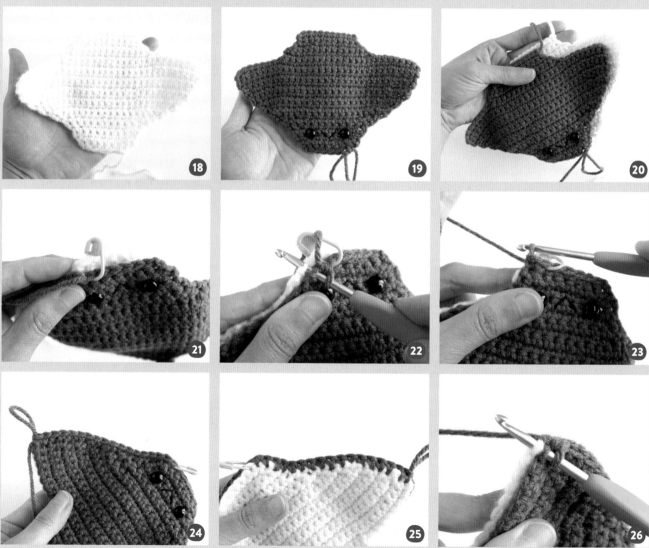

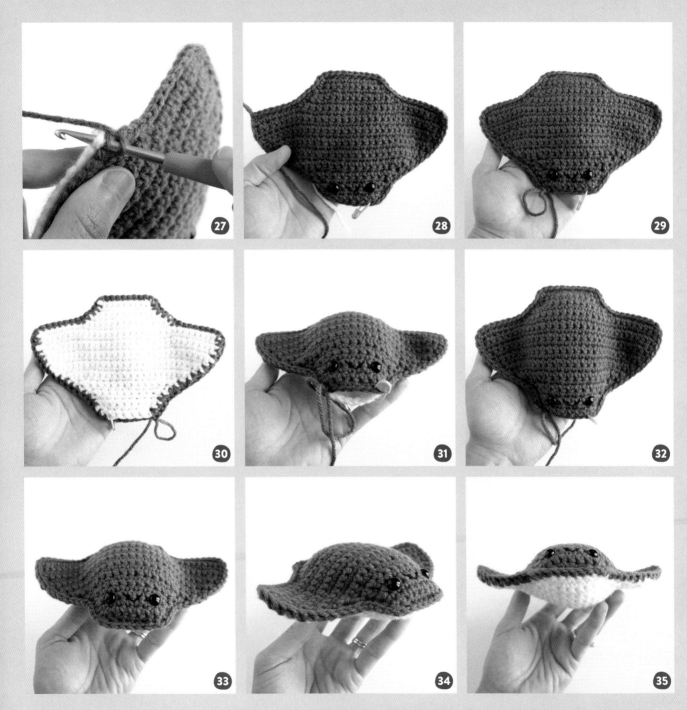

TAIL

Using blue yarn,

R1   6 sc in magic ring. (6 sts)

R2-15   Sc 6.

Fasten off and leave a tail for sewing. Leave the tail unstuffed. (photo 36)

With the yarn needle and the tail, sew the tail to the rear. Make sure to attach it in the center and mainly on the white part. (photos 37-39) Secure with a knot and hide inside the body. (photos 40-42)

Optional:

Use different shades of blues and grays to create an eagle ray or stingray. Use white yarn to create spots for the eagle ray. (photo 43)

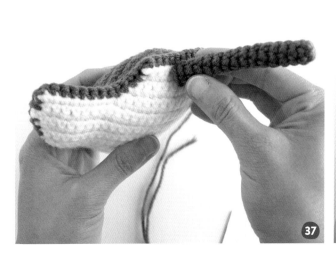

ORCA

INTERMEDIATE

FINISHED MEASUREMENTS
- Approx. 4.5 inches wide by 7 inches tall by 11.5 inches long

MATERIALS
- Worsted weight yarn: Black and White
- Size F/3.75mm crochet hook
- One pair of 10mm safety eyes
- Polyester fiberfill stuffing
- Yarn needle
- Scissors
- Stitch marker
- Straight pins

ABBREVIATIONS
- Ch- Chain
- Dec- Decrease
- Hdc- Half Double Crochet
- Inc- Increase
- Inv Dec- Invisible Decrease
- R- Round/Row
- Sc- Single Crochet
- St/s- Stitch/es

EYE PATCH: MAKE 2

Using white yarn,

R1	6 sc in magic ring. (6 sts)
R2	*Inc, sc 2* 2 times. (8 sts)
R3	*Inc in the next two sts, sc 2* 2 times. (12 sts)

Fasten off and leave a tail for sewing. Set aside. (photo 1)

BODY

Using black yarn,

R1	6 sc in magic ring. (6 sts)
R2	Sc 6.
R3	Inc in each st around. (12 sts)
R4	*Sc 1, inc* 6 times. (18 sts)
R5	*Sc 2, inc* 6 times. (24 sts)
R6	*Sc 3, inc* 6 times. (30 sts)
R7	*Sc 4, inc* 6 times. (36 sts)
R8	Sc 36.
R9	*Sc 5, inc* 6 times. (42 sts)
R10	Sc 42.
R11	*Sc 6, inc* 6 times. (48 sts)
R12	Sc 48.
R13	*Sc 7, inc* 6 times. (54 sts)
R14-31	Sc 54.

After round 22, position the eye patches on either side of the body, between rounds 14-19. (photo 2) The eye patches should be about 20 stitches apart. With the yarn needle and the tail, sew the eye patches to the body. Weave the needle under both loops (the "V") from the stitches on R3 of the eye patch and then into the body. (photos 3+4) Make sure to go under the stitches and not over them to create a clean finish. Secure with a knot and hide inside the body. (photo 5) Add the safety eyes between rounds 14 and 15, placing them right next to the eye patches. (photos 6+7)

R32	*Sc 16, inv dec* 3 times. (51 sts)
R33	Sc 51.

Begin adding fiberfill and continue adding as you close the piece.

R34	*Sc 15, inv dec* 3 times. (48 sts)
R35+36	Sc 48.
R37	*Sc 14, inv dec* 3 times. (45 sts)
R38+39	Sc 45.
R40	*Sc 13, inv dec* 3 times. (42 sts)
R41	Sc 42.
R42	*Sc 12, inv dec* 3 times. (39 sts)
R43	Sc 39.
R44	*Sc 11, inv dec* 3 times. (36 sts)
R45	Sc 36.
R46	*Sc 10, inv dec* 3 times. (33 sts)
R47+48	Sc 33.
R49	*Sc 9, inv dec* 3 times. (30 sts)
R50	Sc 30.
R51	*Sc 3, inv dec* 6 times. (24 sts)
R52	Sc 24.
R53	*Sc 2, inv dec* 6 times. (18 sts)
R54	Sc 18.
R55	*Sc 1, inv dec* 6 times. (12 sts)
R56	Inv dec around 6 times. (6 sts)

Fasten off and leave a tail to close the piece. (photos 8+9)

PECTORAL SIDE FINS: MAKE 2

Using black yarn,

R1	6 sc in magic ring. (6 sts)
R2	Inc in each st around. (12 sts)
R3	Sc 12.
R4	*Sc 1, inc* 6 times. (18 sts)
R5-9	Sc 18.
R10	*Sc 1, inv dec* 6 times. (12 sts)

Fasten off and leave a tail for sewing. Leave fins unstuffed. (photo 10)

Using straight pins, pin the fins on the sides of the body, placing them between rounds 27-34. (photos 11+12) When positioning them, make sure to line the fin up with the bottom of the eye patch. With the yarn needle and the tail, sew the fin to the body. Secure with a knot and hide inside the body. (photo 13)

DORSAL FIN

Using black yarn,

R1	6 sc in magic ring. (6 sts)
R2	Sc 6.
R3	*Sc 1, inc* 3 times. (9 sts)
R4	Sc 9.
R5	*Sc 2, inc* 3 times. (12 sts)
R6	Sc 12.
R7	*Sc 3, inc* 3 times. (15 sts)
R8	Sc 15.
R9	*Sc 4, inc* 3 times. (18 sts)
R10	Sc 18.
R11	*Sc 5, inc* 3 times. (21 sts)
R12	Sc 21.
R13	*Sc 6, inc* 3 times. (24 sts)
R14	Sc 24.

Fasten off and leave a tail for sewing. Leave fin unstuffed. (photo 14)

Using straight pins, pin the fin to the top of the body, placing it between rounds 25-35. (photos 15+16) Make sure the dorsal fin is centered. With the yarn needle and the tail, sew the fin to the body. Secure with a knot and hide inside the body. (photos 17+18)

FLUKE: MAKE 2

Using black yarn,

R1	6 sc in magic ring. (6 sts)
R2	Sc 6.
R3	Inc in each st around. (12 sts)
R4	Sc 12.
R5	*Sc 1, inc* 6 times. (18 sts)
R6	Sc 18.
R7	*Sc 2, inc* 6 times. (24 sts)
R8	Sc 24.
R9	*Sc 2, inv dec* 6 times. (18 sts)
R10	*Sc 1, inv dec* 6 times. (12 sts)
R11	*Sc 2, inv dec* 3 times. (9 sts)

Fasten off and leave a tail for sewing. Leave fluke unstuffed. (photo 19)

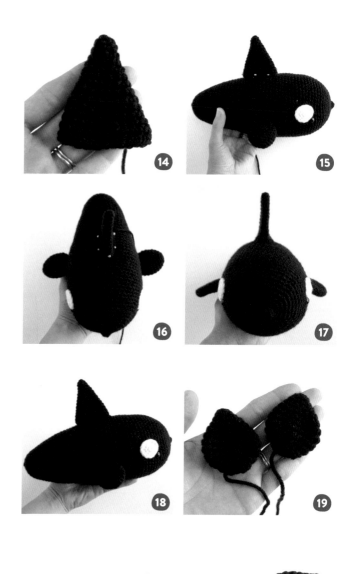

To make the tail, hold both pieces at a slight angle so that rounds 9-11 are touching. (photo 20) With one of the tails left for sewing and the yarn needle, sew the parts of the fins that are touching together, starting at round 11 and working toward round 9. (photo 21) Once you reach round 9, secure the tail with a knot and hide inside the tail. (photo 22) Using straight pins, pin the fluke horizontally to the tail area, near rounds 55 and 56. (photo 23) With the yarn needle and the tail, sew the fluke to the body. (photo 24) Secure with a knot and hide inside the body. (photos 25+26)

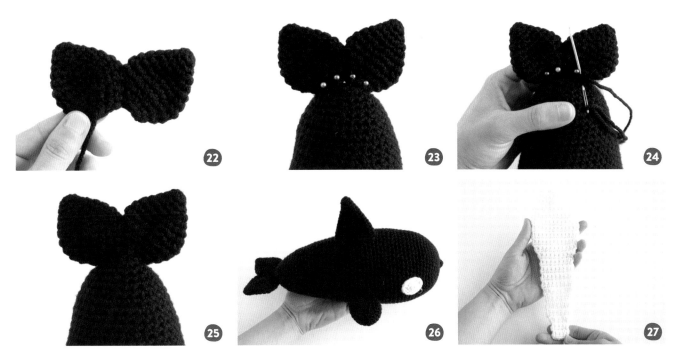

BELLY

Using white yarn,

R1	Ch 2 then in the 2nd ch from hook, inc. (2 sts) Ch 1 and turn.
R2	Inc in each st across. (4 sts) Ch 1 and turn.
R3	Inc, sc 2, inc. (6 sts) Ch 1 and turn.
R4	Inc, sc 4, inc. (8 sts) Ch 1 and turn.
R5	Inc, sc 6, inc. (10 sts) Ch 1 and turn.
R6-8	Sc 10. Ch 1 and turn after each row.
R9	Inc, sc 8, inc. (12 sts) Ch 1 and turn.
R10-19	Sc 12. Ch 1 and turn after each row.
R20	Dec, sc 8, dec. (10 sts) Ch 1 and turn.
R21	Sc 10. Ch 1 and turn.

R22	Dec, sc 6, dec. (8 sts) Ch 1 and turn.
R23-32	Sc 8. Ch 1 and turn after each row.
R33	Dec, sc 4, dec. (6 sts) Ch 1 and turn.
R34-39	Sc 6. Ch 1 and turn after each row.
R40	Dec, sc 2, dec. (4 sts) Ch 1 and turn.
R41-45	Sc 4. Ch 1 and turn after each row, except for row 45. (photo 27)

For this next row we are going to work around the edge of the belly.

R46	Sc in the same st as the last sc. (photo 28) Sc 11, ch 14 then starting in the

2nd ch from hook, hdc in each ch across. (13 sts) (photos 29-32) Sc into the next space along the edge then sc 31. (photos 33+34) You should have reached the tip at this point. Inc in the tip of the belly. (photo 35) Sc 32, ch 14, then, starting in the 2nd ch from hook, hdc in each ch across. (13 sts) (photos 36+37) Sc into the next space along the edge, then sc 11 to the end. You should have 94 stitches at the end, including the 4 sc from row 45. Do not count any of the hdc in the chain pieces.

Fasten off and leave an extra-long tail for sewing.

Using straight pins, pin the belly piece to the body. The tip of the belly will hit right under the nose and the rest will go all the way down to round 52. (photos 38+39) Pin the chained pieces to the sides, curling them to go toward the tail. (photo 40) With the yarn needle and the tail, weave under both loops (the "V") from the stitches on R46 of the belly and into the body. (photos 41+42) Weave the needle back into the body and under the next stitch on the belly piece. (photo 43) When you reach the chained pieces, weave under both loops of the stitches as well. (photos 44-46) Make sure to go under the stitches and not over them to create a clean finish. Secure with a knot and hide inside the body. (photos 47-49)

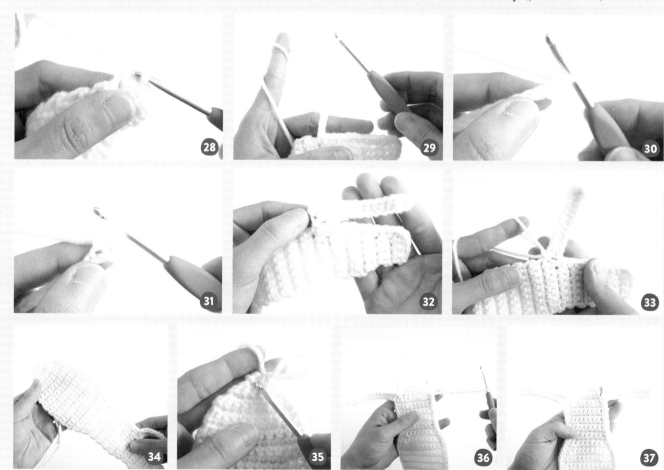

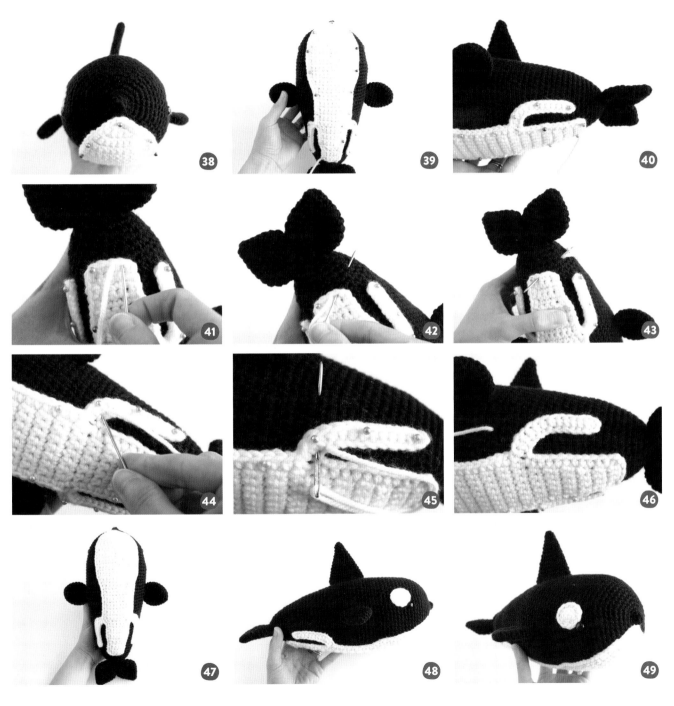

JUNGLE

MONKEY

INTERMEDIATE

FINISHED MEASUREMENTS
- ✂ Approx. 6 inches wide by 10.5 inches tall when standing (7.5 inches tall when sitting)

MATERIALS
- ✂ Worsted weight yarn: Brown and Tan
- ✂ Size F/3.75mm crochet hook
- ✂ One pair of 12mm safety eyes
- ✂ Polyester fiberfill stuffing
- ✂ Yarn needle
- ✂ Scissors
- ✂ Stitch marker
- ✂ Straight pins

ABBREVIATIONS
- ✂ Bo- Bobble
- ✂ Ch- Chain
- ✂ Dc Inc- Double Crochet Increase
- ✂ Hdc Inc- Half Double Crochet Increase
- ✂ Inc- Increase
- ✂ Inv Dec- Invisible Decrease
- ✂ R- Round/Row
- ✂ Sc- Single Crochet
- ✂ St/s- Stitch/es
- ✂ Tr Inc- Treble Crochet Increase

FACE PIECE

Using tan yarn,

R1   Ch 15 then starting in the 2nd ch from hook and in both loops leaving the back "bump", sc in each chain across. (14 sts) Ch 1 and turn. (photos 1-3)

R2   Sc, hdc inc, dc inc, tr inc, dc inc, hdc inc, sc in the next 2 sts, hdc inc, dc inc, tr inc, dc inc, hdc inc, sc. (24 sts) (photos 4+5)

Fasten off and leave a long tail for sewing.

Add the safety eyes between rows 1 and 2, placing them about 6 stitches apart. These will be placed under the treble crochet stitches from row 2. (photos 6+7) Do not attach the safety backings yet. Set face piece aside.

HEAD

Using brown yarn,

R1   6 sc in magic ring. (6 sts)
R2   Inc in each st around. (12 sts)
R3   *Sc 1, inc* 6 times. (18 sts)
R4   *Sc 2, inc* 6 times. (24 sts)
R5   *Sc 3, inc* 6 times. (30 sts)
R6   *Sc 4, inc* 6 times. (36 sts)
R7   *Sc 5, inc* 6 times. (42 sts)
R8   *Sc 6, inc* 6 times. (48 sts)
R9   *Sc 7, inc* 6 times. (54 sts)
R10-18   Sc 54.

Add the safety eyes between rounds 12 and 13, placing them 6 stitches apart. The ends of the face piece should meet rounds 16 and 17. Add the safety backing to the safety eyes. If it's too thick, try flipping the washer and attaching it backwards to the eye post. (photo 8)

With the yarn needle and the tail, sew the face piece to the head. Weave the needle under both loops (the "V") from the stitches on R2 of the face piece and then into the head. (photo 9) Insert the needle into the next stitch and pull the needle through to the outside. (photo 10) Then, going towards the previous stitch, insert the needle under both loops and pull through to the inside of the head. (photo 11) Make sure to go under the stitches and not over them to create a clean finish. Once the top part is sewn into place, sew the back "bumps" left over from R1 to the head. Repeating the same technique for weaving the needle. (photos 12+13) Secure with a knot and hide inside the head. (photo 14)

R19	*Sc 7, inv dec* 6 times. (48 sts)
R20	*Sc 6, inv dec* 6 times. (42 sts)
R21	*Sc 5, inv dec* 6 times. (36 sts)

Begin adding fiberfill and continue adding as you close the piece.

R22	*Sc 4, inv dec* 6 times. (30 sts)
R23	*Sc 3, inv dec* 6 times. (24 sts)
R24	*Sc 2, inv dec* 6 times. (18 sts)
R25	*Sc 1, inv dec* 6 times. (12 sts)
R26	Inv dec around 6 times. (6 sts)

Fasten off and leave a tail to close the piece. (photo 15)

NOSE

Using tan yarn,

R1	6 sc in magic ring. (6 sts)
R2	Inc in each st around. (12 sts)
R3	*Sc 1, inc* 6 times. (18 sts)
R4	*Sc 2, inc* 6 times. (24 sts)
R5	*Sc 3, inc* 6 times. (30 sts)
R6-8	Sc 30.

Fasten off and leave a tail for sewing. (photo 16)

For the nostrils, use about a 15-inch piece of brown yarn. An easy way to find where you want the nostrils is to use straight pins. Place 4 straight pins (2 for each nostril) between rounds 5 and 6. Each nostril will be 3 stitches in length and there will be 3 stitches between each one. (photo 17) Weave the needle over the spot about 5 to 6 times to build up the nostril. (photos 18-20) Secure the yarn with a knot and trim the end. (photo 21)

Using straight pins, pin the nose to the head between rounds 13-22. (photo 22) The nose will fit right under the face piece. With the yarn needle and the tail, sew the nose to the head. Weave the needle under both loops (the "V") from the stitches on R8 of the nose and then into the head, coming out through one of the stitch holes. Insert the needle into the same stitch hole and then go over to the next stitch on the nose and repeat. (photos 23+24) Repeat the same technique for where the nose and face piece meet. (photo 25) Make sure to go under the stitches and not over them to create a clean finish. Make sure to add fiberfill to the nose before closing the piece. Secure with a knot and hide inside the head. (photos 26+27)

EARS: MAKE 2

Using brown yarn,

R1	6 sc in magic ring. (6 sts)
R2	Inc in each st around. (12 sts)
R3	*Sc 1, inc* 6 times. (18 sts)
R4	*Sc 2, inc* 6 times. (24 sts)
R5	*Sc 3, inc* 6 times. (30 sts)
R6	Sc 30.
R7	*Sc 3, inv dec* 6 times. (24 sts)
R8	Sc 24.
R9	*Sc 2, inv dec* 6 times. (18 sts)

Fasten off and leave a tail for sewing. Leave ears unstuffed. (photo 28)

Using straight pins, pin the ears to the head between rounds 9-17. (photos 29+30) The ears should be about 6 stitches away from the face piece. (photo 31) With the yarn needle and the tail, sew the ears in place. Secure with a knot and hide inside the head. (photo 32)

BODY

Using brown yarn,

R1	6 sc in magic ring. (6 sts)
R2	Inc in each st around. (12 sts)
R3	*Sc 1, inc* 6 times. (18 sts)
R4	*Sc 2, inc* 6 times. (24 sts)
R5	*Sc 3, inc* 6 times. (30 sts)
R6	*Sc 4, inc* 6 times. (36 sts)
R7	*Sc 5, inc* 6 times. (42 sts)
R8	*Sc 6, inc* 6 times. (48 sts)
R9	*Sc 7, inc* 6 times. (54 sts)
R10+11	Sc 54.
R12	*Sc 7, inv dec* 6 times. (48 sts)
R13-15	Sc 48.
R16	*Sc 6, inv dec* 6 times. (42 sts)
R17-19	Sc 42.
R20	*Sc 5, inv dec* 6 times. (36 sts)

Begin adding fiberfill and continue adding as you work the piece.

R21-23	Sc 36.
R24	*Sc 4, inv dec* 6 times. (30 sts)
R25-27	Sc 30.

Fasten off and leave a tail for sewing. (photo 33)

Using straight pins, pin the body to the head. (photo 34) With the yarn needle and the tail, sew the head in place on the body. (photo 35) If needed, add any extra fiberfill to the body before closing the piece. Secure with a knot and hide inside the body. (photos 36+37)

BELLY

Using tan yarn,

R1	6 sc in magic ring. (6 sts)
R2	Inc in each st around. (12 sts)
R3	*Sc 1, inc* 6 times. (18 sts)
R4	Sc 1, inc, *Sc 2, inc* 5 times, sc 1. (24 sts)
R5	*Sc 3, inc* 6 times. (30 sts)
R6	Sc 2, inc, *Sc 4, inc* 5 times, sc 2. (36 sts)
R7	*Sc 5, inc* 6 times. (42 sts)

Fasten off and leave a long tail for sewing. (photo 38)

Using straight pins, pin the belly to the body between rounds 11-25. (photo 39) With the yarn needle and the tail, sew the circle to the body. Weave the needle under both loops (the "V") from the stitches on R7 of the belly and then into the body, coming out through one of the stitch holes. (photo 40) Insert the needle into the same stitch hole and then go over to the next stitch on the belly and repeat. (photos 41+42) Make sure to go under the stitches and not over them to create a clean finish. Secure with a knot and hide inside the body. (photo 43)

ARMS: MAKE 2

Using tan yarn,

R1	6 sc in magic ring. (6 sts)
R2	Inc in each st around. (12 sts)
R3	*Sc 1, inc* 6 times. (18 sts)
R4+5	Sc 18.
R6	Sc 4, BO, sc 13. (18 sts) (photos 44+45) When the bobble is complete, push the bobble so it faces outward. (photos 46-48)
R7	Sc 18.
R8	*Sc 1, inv dec* 6 times. (12 sts)

Begin adding fiberfill and continue adding as you work the piece.

Change to brown yarn,

R9-21	Sc 12. (photo 49)
R22	Sc 5. Do this by lining up the stitches on both sides of the arm, then inserting the hook into both stitches. Then sc as normal. (photos 50-53)

Fasten off and leave a tail for sewing. (photo 54)

Using straight pins, pin the arms to the sides of the body between rounds 20-24. (photos 55-57) Make sure to pin the arms at a slight angle with the thumbs pointing up. With the yarn needle and the tail, sew the arms to the body. Weave the needle under both loops (the "V") from R22 of the arms and then into the body. (photos 58-60) Secure with a knot and hide inside the body. (photos 61-63)

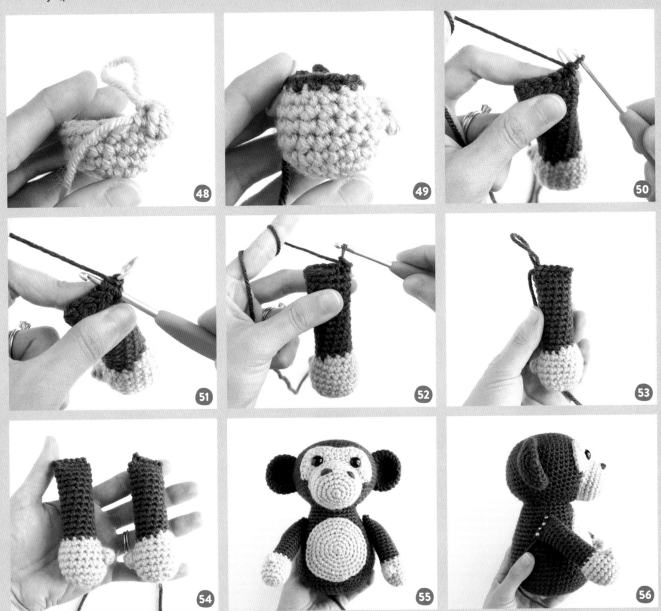

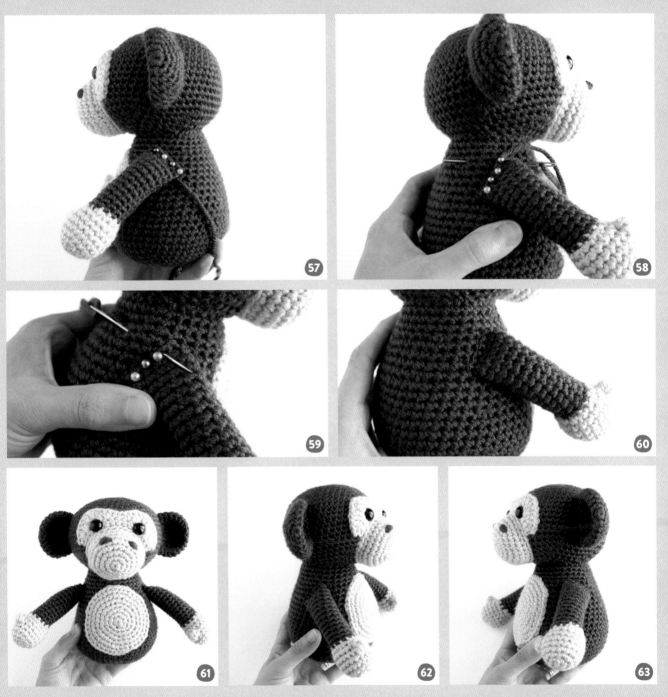

LEGS: MAKE 2

Using tan yarn,

R1	6 sc in magic ring. (6 sts)
R2	Inc in each st around. (12 sts)
R3	*Sc 1, inc* 6 times. (18 sts)
R4+5	Sc 18.

Change to brown yarn,

R6+7	Sc 18.
R8	*Sc 1, inv dec* 6 times. (12 sts) (photo 64)

Begin adding fiberfill and continue adding as you work the piece.

R9-19	Sc 12.
R20	Sc 5. Do this by lining up the stitches on both sides of the leg, then inserting the hook into both stitches. Then sc as normal. (photos 65-68)

Fasten off and leave a tail for sewing. (photo 69)

Using straight pins, pin the legs to the underside of the body between rounds 2-6. (photos 70+71) With the yarn needle and the tail, sew the legs to the body. Weave the needle under both loops (the "V") from R20 of the legs and then into the body. (photos 72-74) Secure with a knot and hide inside the body. (photos 75+76)

TAIL

Using brown yarn,

R1	8 sc in magic ring. (8 sts)
R2-29	Sc 8.

Add fiberfill to the tail as you work each round. Fasten off and leave a tail for sewing. (photo 77)

Using straight pins, pin the tail to the body between rounds 8-10. (photo 78) With the yarn needle and the tail, sew the tail to the body. Bend the tail to form into a wavy "S" shape. (photo 79) Secure with a knot and hide inside the body. (photos 80+81)

SLOTH

BEGINNER

FINISHED MEASUREMENTS
✕ Approx. 6 inches wide by 7.5 inches tall

MATERIALS
✕ Worsted weight yarn: Brown, Tan and Cream
✕ Size F/3.75mm crochet hook
✕ One pair of 10mm safety eyes
✕ Black felt
✕ Black embroidery floss and needle
✕ Polyester fiberfill stuffing
✕ Yarn needle
✕ Scissors
✕ Stitch marker
✕ Straight pins

ABBREVIATIONS
✕ Ch- Chain
✕ Inc- Increase
✕ Inv Dec- Invisible Decrease
✕ R- Round/Row
✕ Sc- Single Crochet
✕ St/s- Stitch/es

EYE PIECES: MAKE 2

Using brown yarn,

R1   Ch 10 then starting in the 2nd ch from hook and in both loops leaving the back "bump", sc in each chain across, 9 times. Turn and then sc across the back "bumps", 9 times. (18 sts) (photos 1-5)

R2   Inc, sc 7, inc in the next two sts, sc 7, inc. (22 sts) (photo 6)

Fasten off and leave a tail for sewing.

Place a safety eye into row 1 of each eye piece. This will be where we single crocheted in both loops and then where we single crocheted in the back "bumps". You'll place the eye in between these stitches. (photos 7+8) Do not attach the safety backings yet.

Set eye pieces aside.

HEAD

Using tan yarn,

R1   6 sc in magic ring. (6 sts)

R2   Inc in each st around. (12 sts)

R3   *Sc 1, inc* 6 times. (18 sts)

R4   Sc 1, inc, *Sc 2, inc* 5 times, sc 1. (24 sts)

R5   *Sc 3, inc* 6 times. (30 sts)

R6   Sc 2, inc, *Sc 4, inc* 5 times, sc 2. (36 sts)

R7   *Sc 5, inc* 6 times. (42 sts)

Change to brown yarn,

R8   Sc 3, inc, *Sc 6, inc* 5 times, sc 3. (48 sts) (photo 9)

R9-17   Sc 48.

Add the safety eyes between rounds 5 and 6, placing them 14 stitches apart. (photo 10)

Tip: Position one of the eye patches so it covers the color change from round 8. (photo 11) Add the safety backing to the safety eyes. If it's too thick, try flipping the washer and attaching it backward to the eye post. (photo 12)

With the yarn needle and the tail, sew the eye pieces to the head. Weave the needle under both loops (the "V") from the stitches on R2 of the eye piece and then into the head. (photos 13+14) To bring the needle back up, insert into the next stitch on the eye piece and pull through. Repeat until you reach the end. Make sure to go under the stitches and not over them to create a clean finish. Secure with a knot and trim tail. (photos 15+16)

With black felt, cut out a small oval nose. (photo 17) Using black embroidery floss, stitch the nose in place on top of the magic ring using a running stitch. (photo 18) With black embroidery floss, sew on the mouth between rounds 3 and 4, about 5 stitches in length. (photo 19)

SLOTH

R18	Sc 3, inv dec, *Sc 6, inv dec* 5 times, sc 3. (42 sts)
R19	*Sc 5, inv dec* 6 times. (36 sts)

Begin adding fiberfill and continue adding as you close the piece.

R20	*Sc 2, inv dec, *Sc 4, inv dec* 5 times, sc 2. (30 sts)
R21	*Sc 3, inv dec* 6 times. (24 sts)
R22	Sc 1, inv dec, *Sc 2, inv dec* 5 times, sc 1. (18 sts)
R23	*Sc 1, inv dec* 6 times. (12 sts)
R24	Inv dec around 6 times. (6 sts)

Fasten off and leave a tail to close the piece. (photos 20+21)

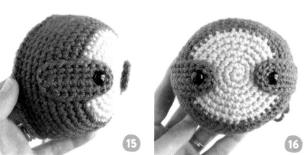

BODY

Using brown yarn,

R1	6 sc in magic ring. (6 sts)
R2	Inc in each st around. (12 sts)
R3	*Sc 1, inc* 6 times. (18 sts)
R4	*Sc 2, inc* 6 times. (24 sts)
R5	*Sc 3, inc* 6 times. (30 sts)
R6	*Sc 4, inc* 6 times. (36 sts)
R7	*Sc 5, inc* 6 times. (42 sts)
R8	*Sc 6, inc* 6 times. (48 sts)
R9	*Sc 7, inc* 6 times. (54 sts)
R10	Sc 54.
R11	*Sc 7, inv dec* 6 times. (48 sts)
R12-14	Sc 48.
R15	*Sc 6, inv dec* 6 times. (42 sts)
R16-18	Sc 42.

Begin adding fiberfill and continue adding as you work the piece.

R19	*Sc 5, inv dec* 6 times. (36 sts)
R20-22	Sc 36.
R23	*Sc 4, inv dec* 6 times. (30 sts)
R24+25	Sc 30.
R26	*Sc 3, inv dec* 6 times. (24 sts)
R27	Sc 24.

Fasten off and leave a tail for sewing. (photo 22)
Using straight pins, pin the body to the head. With the yarn needle, sew the head in place on the body. (photo 23) If needed, add any extra fiberfill to the body before closing the piece. Secure with a knot and hide inside the body. (photos 24+25)

NAILS: MAKE 12

Using cream yarn,

R1   Ch 6 then starting in the 2nd ch from hook sc in each chain across. (5 sts) (photos 26+27)

Fasten off and leave a tail for sewing. (photo 28) Set nails aside.

ARMS: MAKE 2

Using brown yarn,

R1   6 sc in magic ring. (6 sts)
R2   Inc in each st around. (12 sts)
R3   *Sc 1, inc* 6 times. (18 sts)
R4+5   Sc 18.
R6   *Sc 1, inv dec* 6 times. (12 sts)

Begin adding fiberfill and continue adding as you close the piece.

R7-19   Sc 12.
R20   Sc 5. Do this by lining up the stitches on both sides of the arm, then inserting the hook into both stitches. Then sc as normal. (photos 29-32)

Fasten off and leave a tail for sewing. (photo 33)

Using straight pins, pin three nails on the tops of the arms between rounds 2 and 3. (photo 34) With the yarn needle and the tail, sew the nails in place. Secure both the starting tail and sewing tail with a knot and hide inside the arms. (photos 35-37)

Using straight pins, pin the arms to the sides of the body between rounds 17-22. (photos 38+39) With the yarn needle and the tail, sew the arms to the body. Weave the needle under both loops (the "V") from R20 of the arms and then into the body. (photos 40-42)

With the same yarn tail, sew the upper arms to the body. This helps keep the arms closer instead of them being outstretched. (photos 43+44) Weave the needle through the upper and inner part of the arm and then into the body. (photos 45+46) Pull the needle through one of the stitch holes on the body. (photo 47) Then insert into the same stitch hole and weave through to the arm. (photo 48) Repeat until you've sewn across the entire upper arm. Secure with a knot and hide inside the body. (photos 49+50)

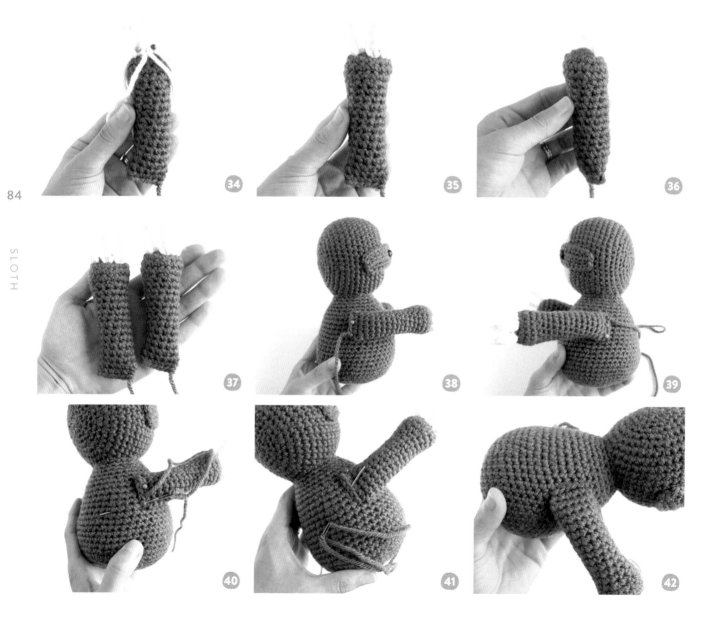

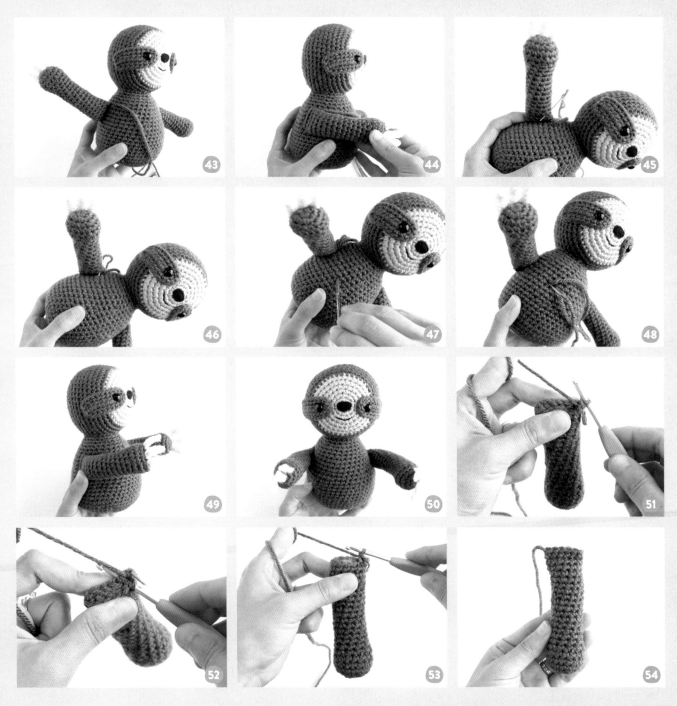

LEGS: MAKE 2

Using brown yarn,

R1	6 sc in magic ring. (6 sts)
R2	Inc in each st around. (12 sts)
R3	*Sc 1, inc* 6 times. (18 sts)
R4+5	Sc 18.
R6	*Sc 1, inv dec* 6 times. (12 sts)

Begin adding fiberfill and continue adding as you close the piece.

R7-22	Sc 12.
R23	Sc 5. Do this by lining up the stitches on both sides of the leg, then inserting the hook into both stitches. Then sc as normal. (photos 51-54)

Fasten off and leave a tail for sewing. (photo 55)

Using straight pins, pin the nails on the tops of the legs between rounds 2 and 3. (photo 56) With the yarn needle and the tail, sew the nails in place. Secure both the starting tail and sewing tail with a knot and hide inside the legs. (photos 57-59)

Using straight pins, pin the legs to the sides of the body between rounds 8-12. Make sure to place them further back than the arms. (photos 60+61) With the yarn needle and the tail, sew the legs to the body. Weave the needle under both loops (the "V") from R23 of the legs and then into the body. (photos 62-64)

With the same yarn tail, sew the upper legs to the body. This will be just like we did for the arms. (photos 65+66) Weave the needle through the upper and inner part of the leg and then into the body. (photo 67) Pull the needle through one of the stitch holes on the body. Then insert into the same stitch hole and weave through to the leg. Repeat until you've sewn across the entire upper leg. (photos 68+69) Secure with a knot and hide inside the body. (photos 70+71)

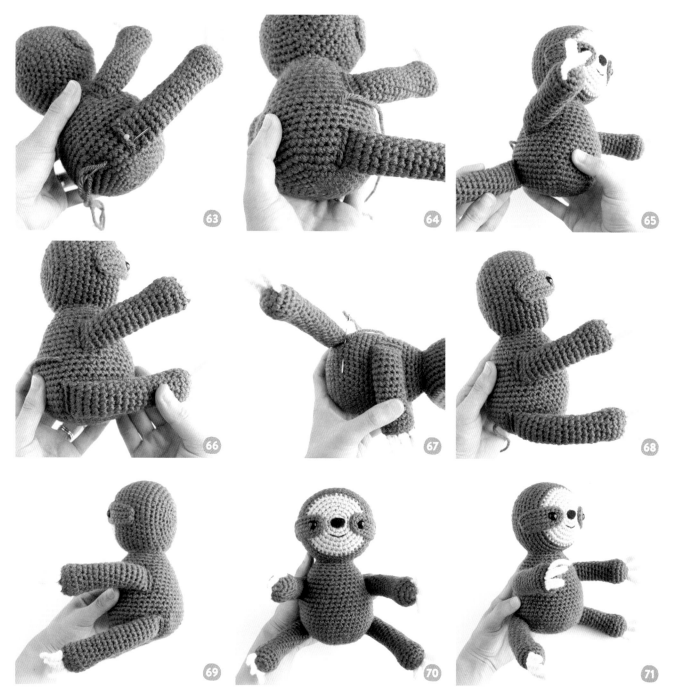

SNAKE

BEGINNER

FINISHED MEASUREMENTS
- Approx. 6 inches wide by 5.5 inches tall

MATERIALS
- Worsted weight yarn: Lime Green and Light Yellow
- Size F/3.75mm crochet hook
- One pair of 10mm safety eyes
- Dark green and pink embroidery floss
- Embroidery needle
- Pink felt
- Polyester fiberfill stuffing
- Yarn needle
- Scissors
- Stitch marker
- Straight pins
- 16-gauge aluminum craft wire- measuring 20 inches
- Tape for the ends of wire

ABBREVIATIONS
- Inc- Increase
- Inv Dec- Invisible Decrease
- R- Round/Row
- Sc- Single Crochet
- St/s- Stitch/es

HEAD

Using lime green yarn,

R1	6 sc in magic ring. (6 sts)
R2	Inc in each st around. (12 sts)
R3	*Sc 1, inc* 6 times. (18 sts)
R4	*Sc 2, inc* 6 times. (24 sts)
R5	*Sc 3, inc* 6 times. (30 sts)
R6	*Sc 4, inc* 6 times. (36 sts)
R7	*Sc 5, inc* 6 times. (42 sts)
R8-12	Sc 42.
R13	*Sc 6, inc* 6 times. (48 sts)
R14	Sc 48.

Add safety eyes between rounds 12 and 13, placing them 6 stitches apart. With dark green embroidery floss, add the nostrils by making two knots on round 12, centered between the eyes. (photo 1) With pink felt, cut a thin strip about 1.5 inches long and then cut a triangle out at the tip. (photo 2) Using pink embroidery floss, sew the tongue under the nostrils between rounds 13 and 14. (photo 3)

Change to light yellow yarn, (photos 4+5)

R15	*Sc 6, inv dec* 6 times. (42 sts) (photo 6)
R16	*Sc 5, inv dec* 6 times. (36 sts)

Begin adding fiberfill and continue adding as you close the piece.

R17	*Sc 4, inv dec* 6 times. (30 sts)
R18	*Sc 3, inv dec* 6 times. (24 sts)
R19	*Sc 2, inv dec* 6 times. (18 sts)
R20	*Sc 1, inv dec* 6 times. (12 sts)
R21	Inv dec around 6 times. (6 sts)

Fasten off and leave a tail to close the piece. (photo 7)

Pinch both sides of the head to create more of a dome shape. (photos 8+9)

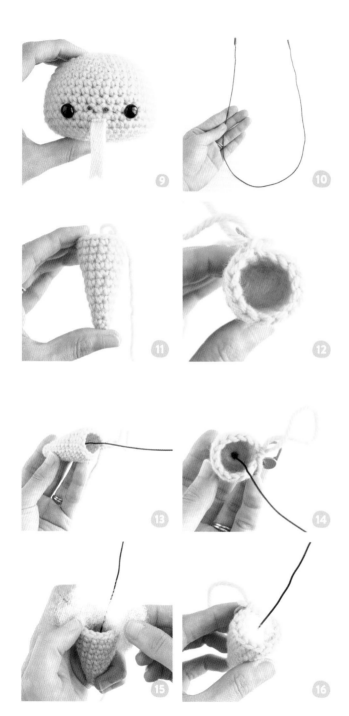

BODY

Note: For safety, add tape to both ends of the wire. (photo 10) *After R12, add a little bit of fiberfill to the tip of the tail.* (photos 11+12) *Then insert the wire into the tail and begin adding fiberfill around it.* (photos 13-15) *You'll want to make sure the wire is centered, so be sure to add the fiberfill around it evenly.* (photo 16) *Continue to crochet each round, adding fiberfill around the wire as you work. If needed, coil the wire into a circle if it's getting in the way as you work.* (photo 17) *Crochet until you reach round 95, or until your piece measures 20 inches (so the wire will fit inside the body).*

Using lime green yarn,

R1	6 sc in magic ring. (6 sts)
R2	Sc 6.
R3	*Sc 1, inc* 3 times. (9 sts)
R4	Sc 9.
R5	*Sc 2, inc* 3 times. (12 sts)
R6+7	Sc 12.
R8	*Sc 3, inc* 3 times. (15 sts)
R9-95	Sc 15. See note above.
R96	*Sc 4, inc* 3 times. (18 sts)
R97	Sc 18.

Change to light yellow yarn, (photo 18)

R98	*Sc 5, inc* 3 times. (21 sts)

Fasten off and leave a tail for sewing. (photo 19)

Using straight pins, pin the body to the head. (photos 20+21) With the yarn needle and the tail, sew the head in place on the body. If needed, add any extra fiberfill to the body before closing the piece. The wire should sit below R98, but if it sticks out, trim or fold the extra wire before attaching the head. Secure the yarn with a knot and hide inside the body. (photos 22-24)

To Assemble: You can coil your snake two ways. The first (version 1) is to twist and tie like a pretzel. The second (version 2) is to coil and sew together.

Version 1: From the neck, leave about 4 inches of the body, then bend so this part stands up. (photo 25) Take the rest of the body and coil counterclockwise. (photo 26) With the tip of the tail, insert into the center of the coil, right behind the 4 inches of neck that were left over. (photo 27) Pull the tail through and then adjust the neck as needed so the snake can stand up by itself. (photos 28-30)

Version 2: Repeat the steps for coiling the body, but instead of tucking the tail into the center, continue coiling the tail around the body. The tip should end on the right side of the snake's body. (photo 31) Cut a long tail of lime green yarn and with the yarn needle, sew the parts of the body that are touching together. (photos 32+33) The tip of the tail and neck should be left unsewn. (photo 34) Secure with a knot and hide inside the body. Bend the tip up slightly and adjust the neck as needed. (photos 35+36)

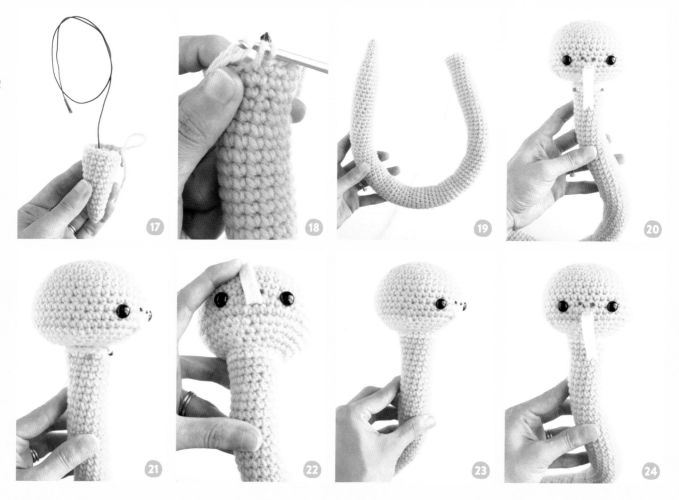

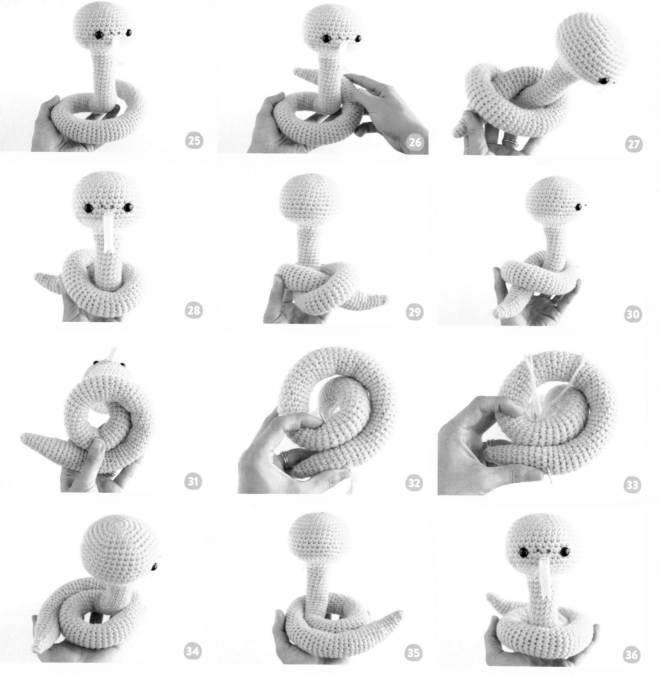

TIGER

✂ ✂ ✂

EXPERT

FINISHED MEASUREMENTS
✂ Approx. 6.5 inches wide by 7 inches tall

MATERIALS
✂ Worsted weight yarn: Orange, Black, and Cream
✂ Size F/3.75mm crochet hook
✂ One pair of 10.5mm safety eyes
✂ Black embroidery floss and needle
✂ Polyester fiberfill stuffing
✂ Yarn needle
✂ Scissors
✂ Stitch marker
✂ Straight pins

ABBREVIATIONS
✂ BLO- Back Loops Only
✂ Inc- Increase
✂ Inv Dec- Invisible Decrease
✂ Mini Bo- Mini Bobble
✂ R- Round/Row
✂ Sc- Single Crochet
✂ St/s- Stitch/es

Note: The tiger has a lot of color changes. I found it best to cut the yarn after each color change and rejoin it when needed. Just make sure to secure all the ends if you do this method. Another option is to carry the yarn behind the work and pick it up when needed. I didn't like this method, as the yarn being carried was visible through the stitches. Remember to leave loose tension on the color not being used if you do this method.

NOSE

Using cream yarn,

R1	6 sc in magic ring. (6 sts)
R2	Inc in each st around. (12 sts)
R3	*Sc 1, inc* 6 times. (18 sts)

Fasten off and leave a tail for sewing. (photo 1)

With black embroidery floss, sew on the black nose. Start below round 3 and stitch completely over round 2 until you reach the magic ring. Next, make one vertical line coming from the bottom center of the nose and meeting at the other side of the magic ring. Then, make two angled lines that meet at the ending point of the vertical line. (photo 2)

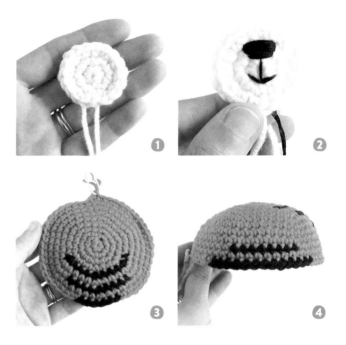

HEAD

Using orange yarn,

R1	6 sc in magic ring. (6 sts)
R2	Inc in each st around. (12 sts)
R3	*Sc 1, inc* 6 times. (18 sts)
R4	*Sc 2, inc* 6 times. (24 sts)
R5	With orange sc 3, inc, sc 3, with black inc, *sc 3, inc* 2 times, sc 1, with orange sc 2, inc, sc 3, inc. (30 sts)
R6	With orange *Sc 4, inc* 6 times. (36 sts)
R7	With orange *Sc 5, inc* 2 times, sc 1, with black sc 4, inc, sc 4, with orange sc 1, inc, *sc 5, inc* 2 times. (42 sts)

R8 With orange *Sc 6, inc* 6 times. (48 sts)

R9 With orange sc 20, with black sc 6, with orange sc 22. (48 sts) (photo 3)

R10+11 With orange sc 48.

R12 With orange sc 7, with black sc 8, with orange sc 18, with black sc 8, with orange sc 7. (48 sts)

R13 With orange sc 48.

R14 With orange sc 5, with black sc 13, with orange sc 13, with black sc 13, with orange sc 4. (48 sts) Fasten off the black yarn. (photo 4)

R15-17 Sc 48.

R18 *Sc 6, inv dec* 6 times. (42 sts)

Add safety eyes between rounds 12 and 13, placing them 8 stitches apart. Make sure to line up the 6 black single crochets from R9 in the center of the eyes. (photo 5)

Position the nose on the head between rounds 11 and 16. (photo 6) With the yarn needle and the tail, sew the nose to the head. Weave the needle under both loops (the "V") from the stitches on R3 of the nose and then into the head. (photo 7) Insert the needle into the next stitch and pull the needle through to the outside. (photo 8) Repeat this technique until you reach the end. Make sure to go under the stitches and not over them to create a clean finish. Secure with a knot and hide inside the head.

R19 *Sc 5, inv dec* 6 times. (36 sts)

Begin adding fiberfill and continue adding as you close the piece.

R20 *Sc 4, inv dec* 6 times. (30 sts)

R21 *Sc 3, inv dec* 6 times. (24 sts)

R22 *Sc 2, inv dec* 6 times. (18 sts)

R23 *Sc 1, inv dec* 6 times. (12 sts)

R24 Inv dec around 6 times. (6 sts)

Fasten off and leave a tail to close the piece. (photos 9+10)

EARS: MAKE 2

Using orange yarn,

R1	6 sc in magic ring. (6 sts)
R2	Inc in each st around. (12 sts)
R3-5	Sc 12.

Fasten off and leave a tail for sewing. Leave ears unstuffed. (photo 11)

Using straight pins, pin the ears to the head between rounds 6 and 10. (photos 12-14) The black stripe from round 5 should be about 1 stitch away. With the yarn needle and the tail, sew the ears to the head. (photo 15) Secure with a knot and hide inside the head. (photo 16)

BODY

Using orange yarn,

R1	6 sc in magic ring. (6 sts)
R2	Inc in each st around. (12 sts)
R3	*Sc 1, inc* 6 times. (18 sts)
R4	*Sc 2, inc* 6 times. (24 sts)
R5	*Sc 3, inc* 6 times. (30 sts)
R6	*Sc 4, inc* 6 times. (36 sts)
R7	*Sc 5, inc* 6 times. (42 sts)
R8	*Sc 6, inc* 6 times. (48 sts)
R9	*Sc 7, inc* 6 times. (54 sts)
R10+11	Sc 54.
R12	*Sc 7, inv dec* 6 times. (48 sts)
R13	With orange sc 8, with black sc 10, with orange sc 14, with black sc 10, with orange sc 6. (48 sts)
R14	With orange sc 48. (photo 17)
R15	With orange sc 6, inv dec, sc 3, with black sc 3, inv dec, sc 6, with orange, inv dec, sc 5, with black sc 1, inv dec, sc 6, inv dec, sc 1, with orange sc 5, inv dec. (42 sts)
R16	With orange sc 42.
R17	With orange sc 7, with black sc 10, with orange sc 13, with black sc 10, with orange sc 2. (42 sts)
R18	With orange sc 42.

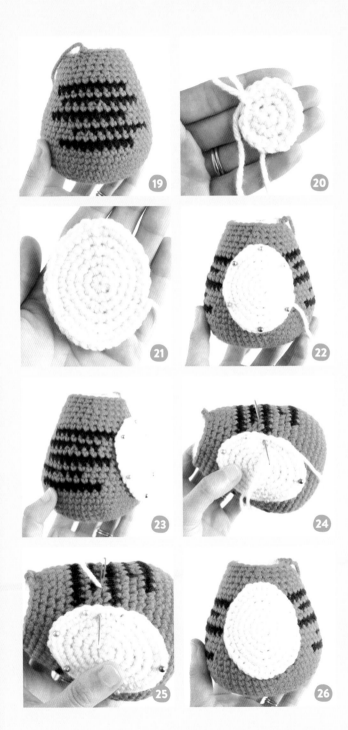

R19 With orange sc 5, inv dec, sc 2, with black sc 3, inv dec, sc 5, inv dec, with orange sc 5, inv dec, with black sc 5, inv dec, sc 4, with orange sc 1, inv dec. (36 sts)

R20 With orange sc 36.

R21 With orange sc 6, with black sc 10, with orange sc 10, with black sc 10. (36 sts)

Change to orange yarn and fasten off the black yarn.

R22 Sc 36.

Begin adding fiberfill and continue adding as you work the piece.

R23 *Sc 4, inv dec* 6 times. (30 sts)

R24+25 Sc 30.

R26 *Sc 3, inv dec* 6 times. (24 sts)

R27 Sc 24.

Fasten off and leave a tail for sewing. (photos 18+19)

BELLY

Using cream yarn,

R1 6 sc in magic ring. (6 sts)

R2 Inc in each st around. (12 sts)

R3 Sc 2, inc in the next three sts, sc 3, inc in the next three sts, sc 1. (18 sts) (photo 20)

R4 Sc 3, inc in the next three sts, sc 6, inc in the next three sts, sc 3. (24 sts)

R5 Sc 5, inc in the next three sts, sc 9, inc in the next three sts, sc 4. (30 sts)

R6 Sc 7, inc in the next three sts, sc 12, inc in the next three sts, sc 5. (36 sts)

Fasten off and leave a tail for sewing. (photo 21)

Using straight pins, pin the belly to the body between rounds 10-24. (photos 22+23) With the yarn needle and the tail, sew the circle to the body. Weave the needle under both loops (the "V") from the stitches on R6 of the belly and then into the body, coming out through one of the stitch holes. (photo 24) Insert the needle into the same stitch hole and then go over to the next stitch on the belly and repeat. (photo 25)

Make sure to go under the stitches and not over them to create a clean finish. Secure with a knot and hide inside the body. (photo 26)

Using straight pins, pin the body to the head between rounds 18-23. Make sure to pin the head at an angle. (photos 27+28) With the yarn needle and the tail, sew the head in place on the body. If needed, add any extra fiberfill to the body before closing the piece. Secure with a knot and hide inside the body. (photos 29+30)

FRONT LEGS: MAKE 2

Using cream yarn,

R1	6 sc in magic ring. (6 sts)	
R2	Inc in each st around. (12 sts)	
R3	*Sc 1, inc* 6 times. (18 sts)	
R4	In BLO, sc 3, mini bo, *sc 1, mini bo* 3 times, sc 8. (18 sts) (photos 31-41)	
R5	*Sc 1, inv dec* 6 times. (12 sts) (photos 42+43)	

Change to orange yarn,

R6-8 Sc 12.

Change to black yarn,

R9 Sc 12.

Change to orange yarn,

R10 Sc 12.

Change to black yarn,

R11 Sc 12.

Change to orange yarn,

R12+13 Sc 12.

Begin adding fiberfill and continue adding as you work the piece.

Change to black yarn,

R14 Sc 12.

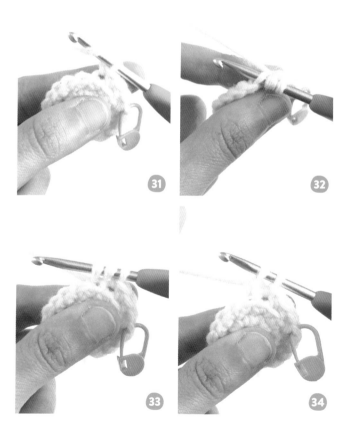

Change to orange yarn,

R15   Sc 12.

Change to black yarn,

R16   Sc 12.

Change to orange yarn,

R17-19   Sc 12.

R20   Sc 5. Do this by lining up the stitches on both sides of the leg, then inserting the hook into both stitches. Then sc as normal. (photos 44-47)

Fasten off and leave a tail for sewing. (photo 48)

Using straight pins, pin the legs to the front of the body near round 24. (photos 49+50) The front legs will go above the belly with the bobbles facing forward. With the yarn needle and the tail, sew the legs to the body. Weave the needle under both loops (the "V") from R20 of the legs and then into the body. (photo 51) Repeat until you reach the end. Secure with a knot and hide inside the body. (photos 52-54)

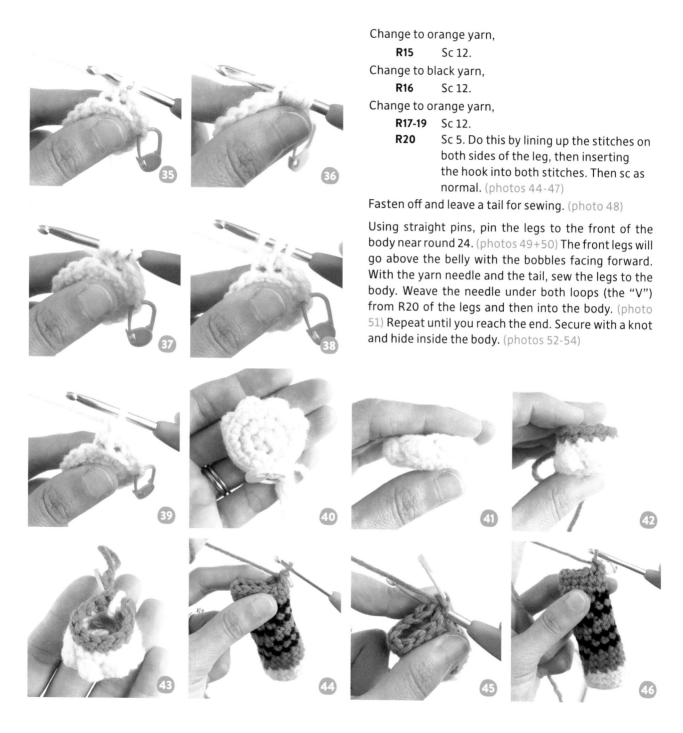

BACK LEGS: MAKE 2

Using cream yarn,

R1	6 sc in magic ring. (6 sts)
R2	Inc in each st around. (12 sts)
R3	*Sc 1, inc* 6 times. (18 sts)
R4	In BLO, sc 4, mini bo, *sc 1, mini bo* 3 times, sc 7. (18 sts) *Note: See front leg photos for reference.*
R5	Sc 18.

Change to orange yarn,

R6	*Sc 1, inv dec* 6 times. (12 sts) (photo 55)
R7+8	Sc 12.

Change to black yarn,

R9	Sc 12.

Change to orange yarn,

R10	Sc 12.

Change to black yarn,

R11	Sc 12.

Change to orange yarn,

R12	Sc 12.

Begin adding fiberfill and continue adding as you work the piece.
Change to black yarn,

R13	Sc 12.

Change to orange yarn,

R14	Sc 12.

Change to black yarn,

R15	Sc 12.

Change to orange yarn,

R16+17	Sc 12.
R18	Sc 1. Next line up the stitches on both sides of the leg then insert the hook into both stitches. Sc across 5 times. This will ensure the toes are pointing up once sewn to body. (photos 56-59)

Fasten off and leave a tail for sewing. (photos 60-62)

Using straight pins, pin the legs to the side of the body between rounds 7-11. (photos 63+64) The bobbles will be facing up. With the yarn needle and the tail, sew the legs to the body. Weave the needle under both loops (the "V") from R18 of the legs and then into the body. (photos 65+66) Repeat until you reach the end. (photo 67)

With the same yarn tail, sew the upper legs to the body. This helps keep the legs closer, instead of outstretched. (photos 68+69) Weave the needle through the upper and inner part of the leg and then into the body. Pull the needle through one of the stitch holes on the body. Then insert into the same stitch hole and weave through to the leg. Repeat until you've sewn across the entire upper leg. Secure with a knot and hide inside the body. (photo 70) *Check out the Sloth pattern for more in-depth photos on this step.*

TAIL

Using black yarn,

R1	5 sc in magic ring. (5 sts)
R2	Inc in each st around. (10 sts)
R3+4	Sc 10.

Change to orange yarn,

R5-7	Sc 10.

Change to black yarn,

R8	Sc 10.

Change to orange yarn,

R9+10	Sc 10.

Change to black yarn,

R11	Sc 10.

Change to orange yarn,

R12+13	Sc 10.

Begin adding fiberfill and continue adding as you work the piece.
Change to black yarn,

R14	Sc 10.

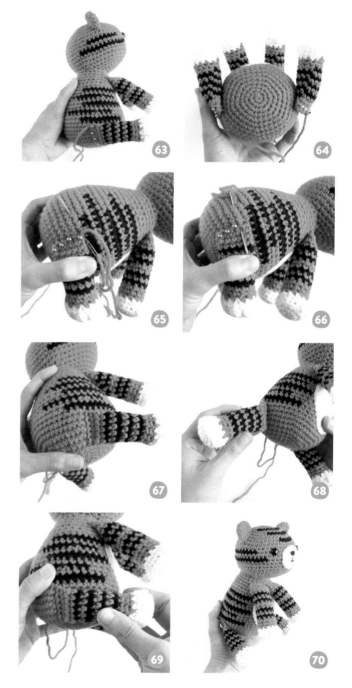

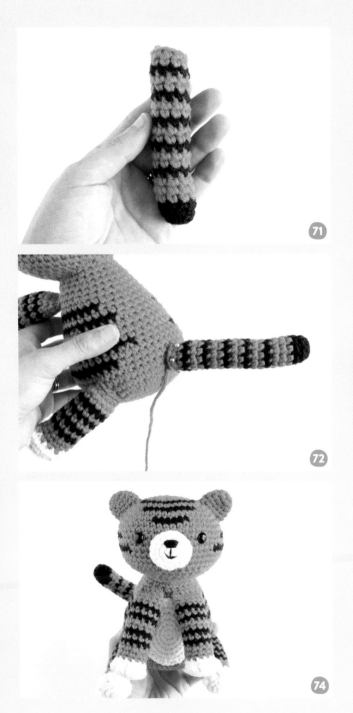

Change to orange yarn,
> **R15+16**   Sc 10.

Change to black yarn,
> **R17**   Sc 10.

Change to orange yarn,
> **R18+19**   Sc 10.

Change to black yarn,
> **R20**   Sc 10.

Change to orange yarn and fasten off the black yarn,
> **R21+22**   Sc 10.

Fasten off and leave a tail for sewing. (photo 71)

Using straight pins, pin the tail to the body between rounds 9-12. (photo 72) With the yarn needle and the tail, sew the tail to the body. Secure with a knot and hide inside the body. (photos 73-75)

TOUCAN

EXPERT

FINISHED MEASUREMENTS
  - Approx. 6.5 inches wide by 7.5 inches tall

MATERIALS
  - Worsted weight yarn: Black, White, Red, Orange, Yellow, Lime Green, Blue, and Light Blue
  - Size F/3.75mm crochet hook
  - One pair of 10mm safety eyes
  - Lime green felt
  - Polyester fiberfill stuffing
  - Yarn needle
  - Scissors
  - Stitch marker
  - Straight pins

ABBREVIATIONS
  - Ch- Chain
  - Dec- Decrease
  - Inc- Increase
  - Inv Dec- Invisible Decrease
  - R- Round/Row
  - Sc- Single Crochet
  - St/s- Stitch/es

BODY

Using black yarn,

R1	6 sc in magic ring. (6 sts)
R2	Inc in each st around. (12 sts)
R3	*Sc 1, inc* 6 times. (18 sts)
R4	*Sc 2, inc* 6 times. (24 sts)
R5	*Sc 3, inc* 6 times. (30 sts)
R6	*Sc 4, inc* 6 times. (36 sts)
R7	*Sc 5, inc* 6 times. (42 sts)
R8	*Sc 6, inc* 6 times. (48 sts)
R9-18	Sc 48.
R19	*Sc 7, inc* 6 times. (54 sts)
R20	Sc 54.
R21	*Sc 8, inc* 6 times. (60 sts)
R22	Sc 60.
R23	*Sc 9, inc* 6 times. (66 sts)
R24-28	Sc 66.
R29	*Sc 9, inv dec* 6 times. (60 sts)
R30	Sc 60.
R31	*Sc 8, inv dec* 6 times. (54 sts)
R32	Sc 54.
R33	*Sc 7, inv dec* 6 times. (48 sts)
R34	Sc 48.
R35	*Sc 6, inv dec* 6 times. (42 sts)

Begin adding fiberfill and continue adding as you close the piece.

R36	*Sc 5, inv dec* 6 times. (36 sts)
R37	*Sc 4, inv dec* 6 times. (30 sts)
R38	*Sc 3, inv dec* 6 times. (24 sts)
R39	*Sc 2, inv dec* 6 times. (18 sts)
R40	*Sc 1, inv dec* 6 times. (12 sts)
R41	Inv dec around 6 times. (6 sts)

Fasten off and leave a tail to close the piece. (photo 1)

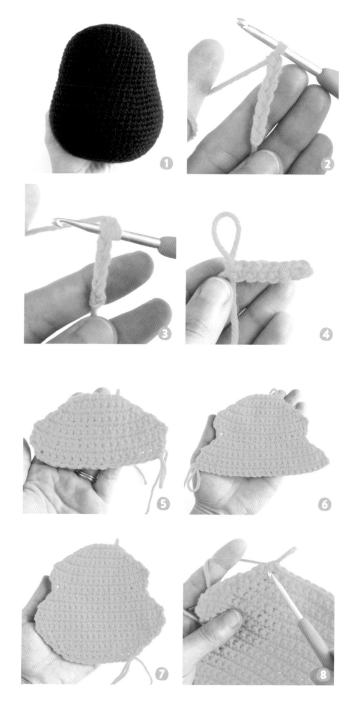

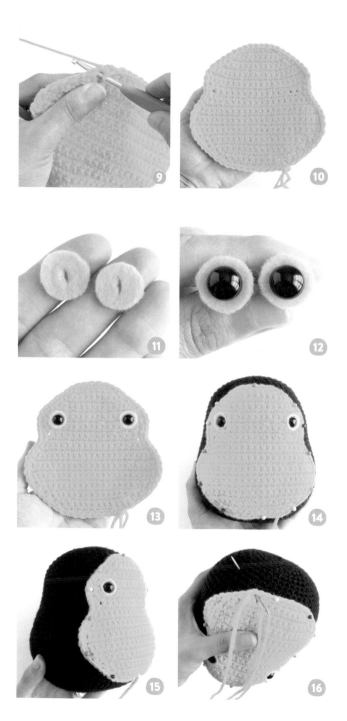

BELLY

Using yellow yarn,

R1	Ch 7 then starting in the 2nd ch from hook and in both loops leaving the back "bump", inc, sc 4, inc. (8 sts) Ch 1 and turn. (photos 2-4)
R2	Inc, sc 6, inc. (10 sts) Ch 1 and turn.
R3	Inc, sc 8, inc. (12 sts) Ch 1 and turn.
R4	Inc, sc 10, inc. (14 sts) Ch 1 and turn.
R5	Inc, sc 12, inc. (16 sts) Ch 1 and turn.
R6	Inc, sc 14, inc. (18 sts) Ch 1 and turn.
R7	Inc, sc 16, inc. (20 sts) Ch 1 and turn.
R8	Sc 20. Ch 1 and turn.
R9	Dec, sc 16, dec. (18 sts) Ch 1 and turn.
R10	Dec, sc 14, dec. (16 sts) Ch 1 and turn.
R11	Sc 16. Ch 1 and turn. (photo 5)
R12	Inc, sc 14, inc. (18 sts) Ch 1 and turn.
R13	Inc, sc 16, inc. (20 sts) Ch 1 and turn.
R14	Inc, sc 18, inc. (22 sts) Ch 1 and turn.
R15	Inc, sc 20, inc. (24 sts) Ch 1 and turn.
R16-18	Sc 24. Ch 1 and turn. (photo 6)
R19	Dec, sc 20, dec. (22 sts) Ch 1 and turn.
R20	Dec, sc 18, dec. (20 sts) Ch 1 and turn.
R21	Dec, sc 16, dec. (18 sts) Ch 1 and turn.
R22	Dec, sc 14, dec. (16 sts) Ch 1 and turn.
R23	Dec, sc 12, dec. (14 sts) Ch 1 and turn.
R24	Dec, sc 10, dec. (12 sts) Ch 1 and turn.
R25	Dec, sc 8, dec. (10 sts) (photo 7)

For this next row we are going to work around the edge of the belly. Place a stitch marker in the last single crochet. This helps keep track of where you'll need to crochet to.

R26	Sc in the same st as the last sc, then continue single crocheting all the way around the edge. Then sc 10 across the stitches from row 25. (64 sts) (photos 8-10)

Fasten off and leave an extra-long tail for sewing.

With lime green felt, cut out two small circles, a little larger than the safety eyes. Cut a very small slit in the center and insert the safety eyes. Do not attach the safety backing yet. (photos 11+12) Place the safety eyes between rows 7 and 8 on the belly, placing them 12 stitches apart. Once in place, attach the safety backings. (photo 13)

Using straight pins, pin the belly to the body between rounds 8-32. (photos 14+15) With the yarn needle and the tail, sew the belly to the body. Weave the needle under both loops (the "V") from the stitches on R26 of the belly and then into the body, coming out through one of the stitch holes. (photos 16+17) Insert the needle into the same stitch hole and then go over to the next stitch on the belly and repeat. Make sure to go under the stitches and not over them to create a clean finish. Secure with a knot and hide inside the body. (photos 18+19)

BEAK

Note: The beak has a lot of color changes. I found it best to carry the yarn behind the round of stitches so that it can be picked up and dropped when needed. Remember to leave loose tension on the yarn being carried. You can also cut and rejoin the yarn if you prefer that method.

Using red yarn,

R1	6 sc in magic ring. (6 sts)
R2	Sc 6.
R3	*Sc 1, inc* 3 times. (9 sts)
R4	*Sc 2, inc* 3 times. (12 sts)
R5	*Sc 3, inc* 3 times. (15 sts) (photo 20)

Change to blue yarn, (photo 21)

R6	Sc 7, with red sc 8. (15 sts) (photos 22+23)

Change to blue yarn,

R7	Sc 4, inc, sc 2, with red sc 2, inc, sc 4, inc. (18 sts)

Change to blue yarn and fasten off the red yarn.

R8	Sc 8, with orange sc 1, with green sc 8, with orange sc 1. (18 sts) (photos 24+25)

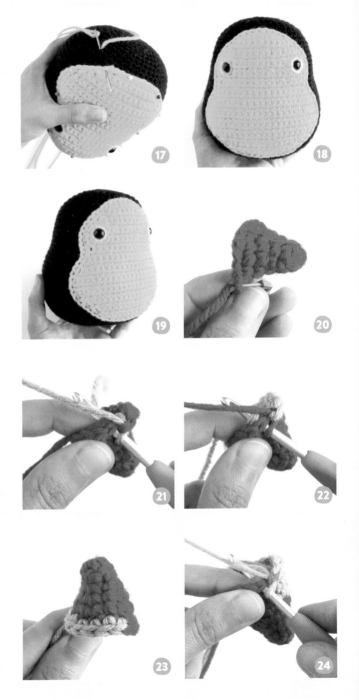

Change to blue yarn,

R9 Sc 5, inc, sc 2, with orange sc 1, with green sc 2, inc, sc 5, inc by making 1 sc in green, then change to orange yarn and sc 1. **(21 sts)** (photo 26)

Change to blue yarn,

R10 Sc 9, with orange sc 1, with green sc 10, with orange sc 1. **(21 sts)**

Change to blue yarn,

R11 Sc 2, with green sc 5, with blue sc 2, with orange sc 1, with green sc 10, with orange sc 1. **(21 sts)** (photo 27)

Change to blue yarn,

R12 Sc 1, with green sc 5, inc, sc 1, with blue sc 1, with orange sc 1, with green sc 3, inc, sc 6, inc by making 1 sc in green then change to orange yarn and sc 1. **(24 sts)** (photo 28)

Change to green yarn and fasten off the blue yarn.

R13 Sc 10, with orange sc 2, with green sc 10, with orange sc 2. **(24 sts)**

Change to green yarn,

R14+15 Sc 10, with orange sc 3, with green sc 8, with orange sc 3. **(24 sts)** (photo 29)

Change to green yarn and fasten off the orange yarn.

R16+17 Sc 24.

Change to black yarn and fasten off the green yarn.

R18 Sc 24.

Fasten off and leave a tail for sewing. Add fiberfill to the beak. (photos 30+31)

Using straight pins, pin the beak to the belly between rows 5-13. (photo 32) With the yarn needle and the tail, sew the beak to the belly. Weave the needle under both loops (the "V") from R18 of the beak and then into the belly only. (photo 33) Repeat until you reach the end, adding any extra fiberfill to the beak before closing the piece. Secure with a knot and hide inside the beak. (photos 34+35)

WINGS: MAKE 2

Using black yarn,

R1	6 sc in magic ring. (6 sts)
R2	*Sc 1, inc* 3 times. (9 sts)
R3	*Sc 2, inc* 3 times. (12 sts)
R4	*Sc 3, inc* 3 times. (15 sts)
R5	Sc 15.
R6	*Sc 4, inc* 3 times. (18 sts)
R7	Sc 18.
R8	*Sc 5, inc* 3 times. (21 sts)
R9	Sc 21.
R10	*Sc 6, inc* 3 times. (24 sts)
R11	Sc 24.
R12	*Sc 7, inc* 3 times. (27 sts)
R13	*Sc 8, inc* 3 times. (30 sts)
R14	*Sc 8, inv dec* 3 times. (27 sts)
R15	*Sc 7, inv dec* 3 times. (24 sts)
R16	*Sc 6, inv dec* 3 times. (21 sts)
R17	*Sc 5, inv dec* 3 times. (18 sts)
R18	*Sc 1, inv dec* 6 times. (12 sts) (photo 36)
R19	Sc 5. Do this by lining up the stitches on both sides of the wing then inserting the hook into both stitches. Then sc as normal. (photos 37+38)

Fasten off and leave a tail for sewing. Leave wings unstuffed. (photos 39+40)

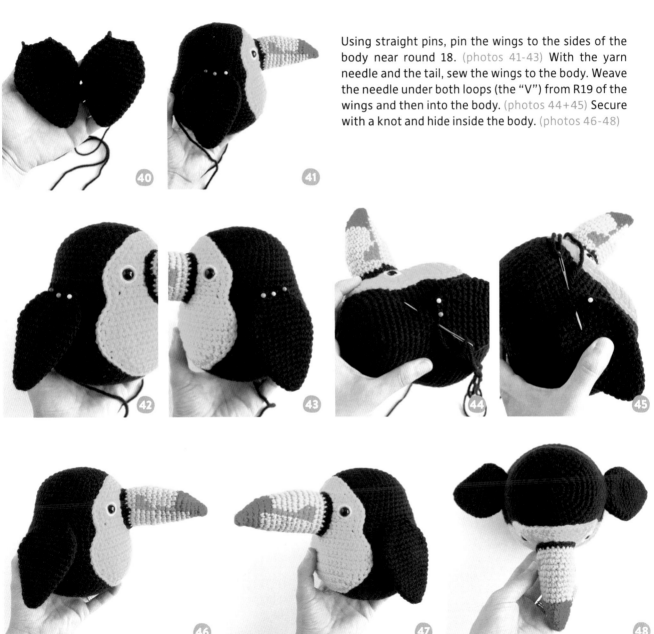

Using straight pins, pin the wings to the sides of the body near round 18. (photos 41-43) With the yarn needle and the tail, sew the wings to the body. Weave the needle under both loops (the "V") from R19 of the wings and then into the body. (photos 44+45) Secure with a knot and hide inside the body. (photos 46-48)

TAIL

Note: The tail has a few color changes. I found it best to cut the yarn after every color change and rejoin when needed. When carrying the red yarn, it was visible behind the white yarn. Cutting and rejoining worked best, but do what method you prefer.

Using white yarn,

R1 Ch 11 then starting in the 2nd ch from hook and in both loops leaving the back "bump" sc in each chain across, 10 times. Change to red yarn and sc across the back bumps, 10 times. (20 sts) (photos 49-55)

Change to white yarn,

R2 Inc, sc 8, inc, with red inc, sc 8, inc. (24 sts) (photo 56)

R3 Inc by making 1 sc in red, then change to white yarn and sc 1, inc, sc 9, inc, inc by making 1 sc in white, then change to red yarn and sc 1, inc, sc 9, inc. (30 sts) (photos 57-59)

R4 Sc 1, with white sc 15, with red sc 14. (30 sts)

R5 Inv dec, with white inv dec, sc 9, inv dec 2 times, with red inv dec, sc 9, inv dec. (24 sts) (photos 60-66)

Fasten off and leave a long tail in both red and white for sewing. (photos 67+68)

Using straight pins, pin the tail to the body near rounds 27-32. (photos 69+70) Starting with the white yarn tail, weave the needle under both loops (the "V") from the stitches on R5 of the tail and then into the body, coming out through one of the stitch holes. (photo 71) Insert the needle into the same stitch hole and go over to the next stitch on the tail piece and repeat. (photo 72) Make sure to go under the stitches and not over them to create a clean finish. Secure the white tail with a knot and hide inside the tail. Add fiberfill to the tail. With the red tail and yarn needle, repeat for attaching the red section to the body. Once you reach the end, secure with a knot and hide inside the tail. (photos 73+74)

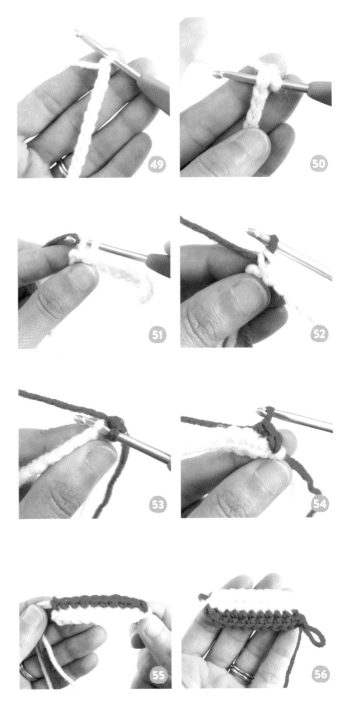

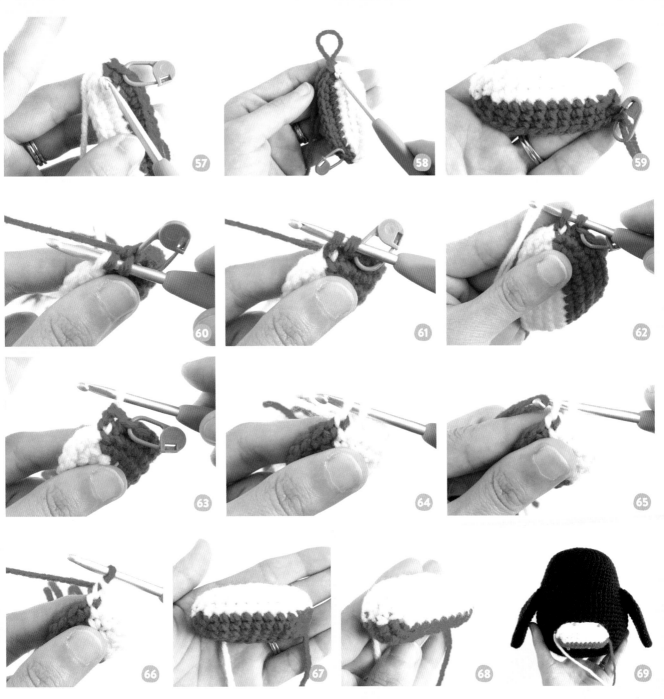

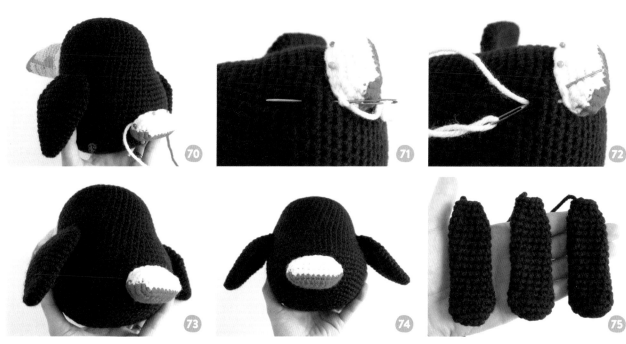

TAIL FEATHERS: MAKE 3

Using black yarn,

R1	6 sc in magic ring. (6 sts)
R2	Inc in each st around. (12 sts)
R3	*Sc 1, inc* 6 times. (18 sts)
R4	Sc 18.
R5	*Sc 1, inv dec* 6 times. (12 sts)
R6-16	Sc 12.
R17	*Sc 2, inv dec* 3 times. (9 sts)
R18	Sc 9.

Fasten off and leave a tail for sewing. Leave feathers unstuffed. (photo 75)

Using straight pins, pin the feathers to the tail piece, placing them right on the line of where the white and red yarn meet. The feathers will go right next to each other. (photos 76+77) With the yarn needle and the tail, sew each feather into place. Secure with a knot and hide inside the tail. (photo 78)

LEGS: MAKE 2

Using light blue yarn,

R1 6 sc in magic ring. (6 sts)

R2-4 Sc 6.

Change to black yarn,

R5 *Sc 1, inc* 3 times. (9 sts)

R6+7 Sc 9.

Fasten off both colors, leaving a black tail for sewing. Secure the light blue yarn. (photo 79)

CLAWS: MAKE 6

Using light blue yarn,

R1 Ch 5 then starting in the 2nd ch from hook, sc in each chain across. (4 sts) (photos 80-82)

Fasten off and leave a tail for sewing. (photo 83)

With the yarn needle, sew two claws next to each other near the magic ring of the leg. This will be the front of the foot. Then sew the last claw on the back of the foot. When looking from the underside of the foot, the claws will look like a "Y". (photo 84) Secure each claw with a knot and hide the ends inside the leg. (photo 85) Add a little bit of fiberfill to the legs.

Using straight pins, pin the legs to the body near rounds 38-40. (photos 86+87) With the yarn needle and the black yarn tail, sew the legs into place. Secure with a knot and hide inside the body. (photos 88+89)

FOREST

FOX

EXPERT

FINISHED MEASUREMENTS
- ✕ Approx. 7.5 inches wide by 7.5 inches tall by 8 inches long

MATERIALS
- ✕ Worsted weight yarn: Orange, Black, and Cream
- ✕ Size F/3.75mm crochet hook
- ✕ One pair of 10.5mm safety eyes
- ✕ Polyester fiberfill stuffing
- ✕ Yarn needle
- ✕ Scissors
- ✕ Stitch marker
- ✕ Straight pins

ABBREVIATIONS
- ✕ Ch- Chain
- ✕ Inc- Increase
- ✕ Inv Dec- Invisible Decrease
- ✕ R- Round/Row
- ✕ Sc- Single Crochet
- ✕ St/s- Stitch/es

HEAD

Using orange yarn,

R1	6 sc in magic ring. (6 sts)
R2	Inc in each st around. (12 sts)
R3	*Sc 1, inc* 6 times. (18 sts)
R4	*Sc 2, inc* 6 times. (24 sts)
R5	*Sc 3, inc* 6 times. (30 sts)
R6	*Sc 4, inc* 6 times. (36 sts)
R7	*Sc 5, inc* 6 times. (42 sts)
R8	*Sc 6, inc* 6 times. (48 sts)
R9	*Sc 7, inc* 6 times. (54 sts)
R10-15	Sc 54.
R16	Sc 12, inc in the next six sts, sc 18, inc in the next six sts, sc 12. (66 sts)

Change to cream yarn,

R17+18	Sc 66.

Add the safety eyes between rounds 15 and 16, placing them about 8 stitches apart. Make sure to center the safety eyes in between the two cheeks that were made in round 16.

R19	Sc 12, inv dec 6 times, sc 18, inv dec 6 times, sc 12. (54 sts)
R20	*Sc 7, inv dec* 6 times. (48 sts)
R21	*Sc 6, inv dec* 6 times. (42 sts)
R22	*Sc 5, inv dec* 6 times. (36 sts)

Begin adding fiberfill and continue adding as you close the piece. Make sure to add more fiberfill to fill out the cheek areas on the sides of the head.

R23	*Sc 4, inv dec* 6 times. (30 sts)
R24	*Sc 3, inv dec* 6 times. (24 sts)
R25	*Sc 2, inv dec* 6 times. (18 sts)
R26	*Sc 1, inv dec* 6 times. (12 sts)
R27	Inv dec around 6 times. (6 sts)

Fasten off and leave a tail to close the piece. (photo 1)

NOSE

Using orange yarn,

R1	6 sc in magic ring. (6 sts)
R2	*Sc 1, inc* 3 times. (9 sts)
R3	*Sc 2, inc* 3 times. (12 sts)
R4	Sc 12.
R5	*Sc 3, inc* 3 times. (15 sts)
R6	Sc 15.
R7	*Sc 4, inc* 3 times. (18 sts)
R8+9	Sc 18.

Fasten off and leave a tail for sewing. (photo 2)

With black yarn, sew a nose over round 2. Go over the spot about 6 times to build up the nose. (photo 3) Secure with a knot and trim the end. Add fiberfill to the nose. Then, using straight pins, pin the nose to the head between rounds 13-19. With the yarn needle and the tail, sew the nose to the head. Secure with a knot and hide inside the head. (photos 4+5)

EARS: MAKE 2

Using black yarn,

R1	6 sc in magic ring. (6 sts)
R2	Sc 6.
R3	*Sc 1, inc* 3 times. (9 sts)
R4	*Sc 2, inc* 3 times. (12 sts)

Change to orange yarn,

R5	*Sc 3, inc* 3 times. (15 sts)
R6	Sc 15.
R7	*Sc 4, inc* 3 times. (18 sts)
R8	Sc 18.
R9	*Sc 5, inc* 3 times. (21 sts)
R10	Sc 21.

Fasten off and leave a tail for sewing. Leave ears unstuffed. (photo 6)

Using straight pins, pin the ears to the head between rounds 4-12. With the yarn needle and the tail, sew the ears in place. Secure with a knot and hide inside the head. (photos 7-9)

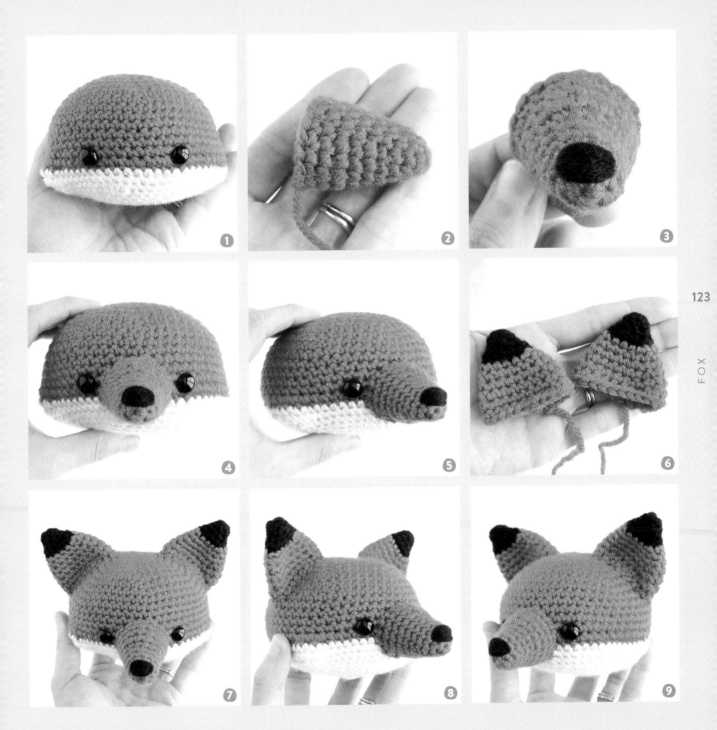

BODY

Using orange yarn,

R1	6 sc in magic ring. (6 sts)
R2	Inc in each st around. (12 sts)
R3	*Sc 1, inc* 6 times. (18 sts)
R4	*Sc 2, inc* 6 times. (24 sts)
R5	*Sc 3, inc* 6 times. (30 sts)
R6	*Sc 4, inc* 6 times. (36 sts)
R7	*Sc 5, inc* 6 times. (42 sts)
R8	*Sc 6, inc* 6 times. (48 sts)
R9	*Sc 7, inc* 6 times. (54 sts)
R10	*Sc 8, inc* 6 times. (60 sts)
R11-13	Sc 60.
R14	*Sc 8, inv dec* 6 times. (54 sts)
R15+16	Sc 54.
R17	*Sc 7, inv dec* 6 times. (48 sts)
R18-20	Sc 48.
R21	*Sc 6, inv dec* 6 times. (42 sts)
R22-24	Sc 42.

Begin adding fiberfill and continue adding as you work the piece.

R25	*Sc 5, inv dec* 6 times. (36 sts)
R26-28	Sc 36.
R29	*Sc 4, inv dec* 6 times. (30 sts)

Fasten off and leave a tail for sewing. (photo 10)

CHEST

Using cream yarn,

R1	Ch 2 then in the 2nd ch from hook, inc. (2 sts) Ch 1 and turn. (photos 11+12)
R2	Inc in each st across. (4 sts) Ch 1 and turn.
R3	Inc, sc 2, inc. (6 sts) Ch 1 and turn.
R4	Sc 6. Ch 1 and turn.
R5	Inc, sc 4, inc. (8 sts) Ch 1 and turn.
R6	Sc 8. Ch 1 and turn.
R7	Inc, sc 6, inc. (10 sts) Ch 1 and turn.
R8	Sc 10. Ch 1 and turn.
R9	Inc, sc 8, inc. (12 sts) Ch 1 and turn.
R10	Sc 12. (photo 13)

For this next row we are going to work around the edge of the piece.

R11	Sc in the same st as the last sc, then continue single crocheting along the two edges until you meet the first sc of R10. (31 sts, including the 12 from R10) (photos 14+15)

Fasten off and leave a long tail for sewing.

Using straight pins, pin the chest piece to the body between rounds 15-26. With the yarn needle and the tail, sew the piece to the body. Weave the needle under both loops (the "V") from the stitches on R11 of the chest piece and then into the body, coming out through one of the stitch holes. Insert the needle into the same stitch hole and then go over to the next stitch on the chest piece and repeat. Make sure to go under the stitches and not over them to create a clean finish. (photos 16+17) Secure with a knot and hide inside the body. (photo 18)

Using straight pins, pin the body to the head. With the yarn needle and the tail, sew the head in place on the body. If needed, add any extra fiberfill to the body before closing the piece. Secure with a knot and hide inside the body. (photos 19-21)

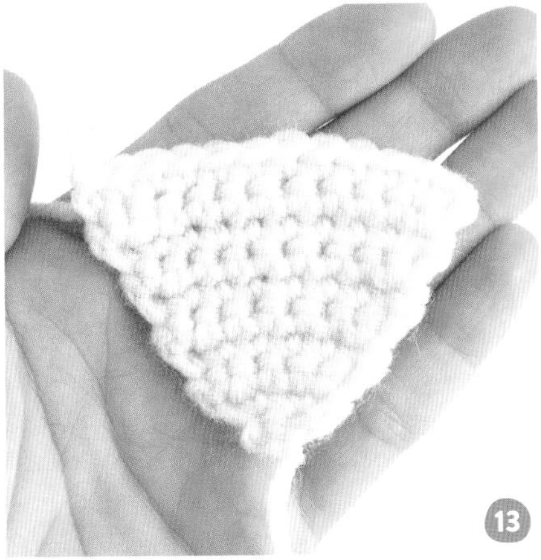
13

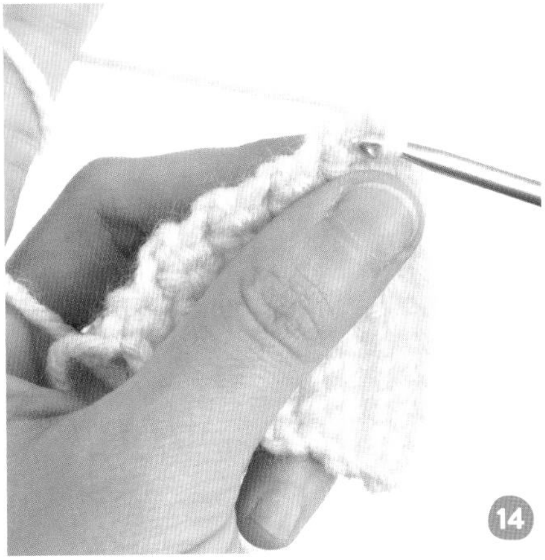
14

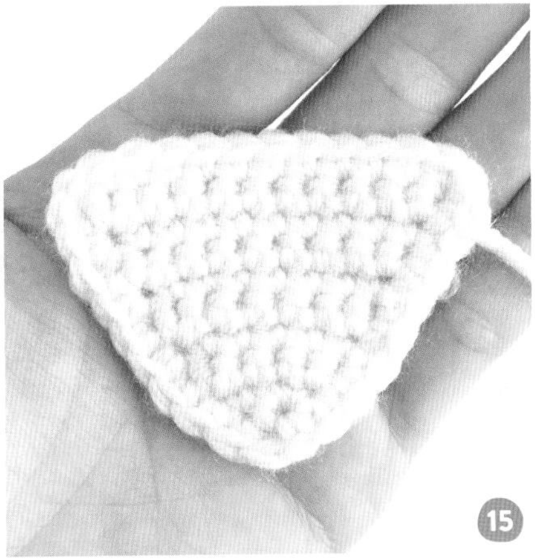
15

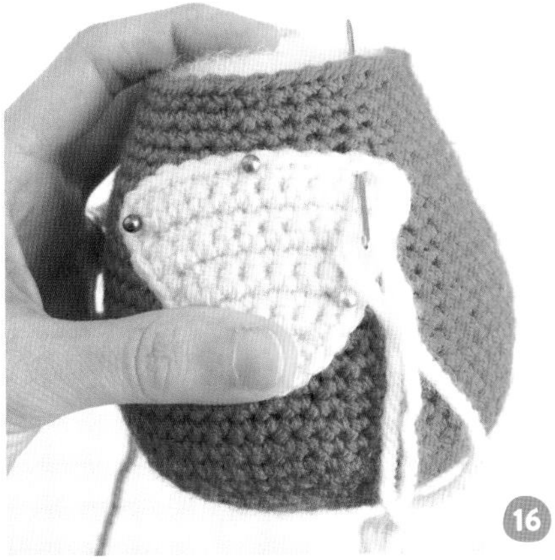
16

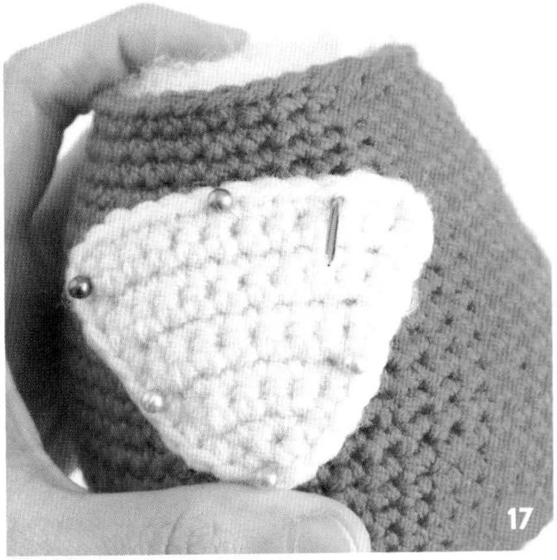
17

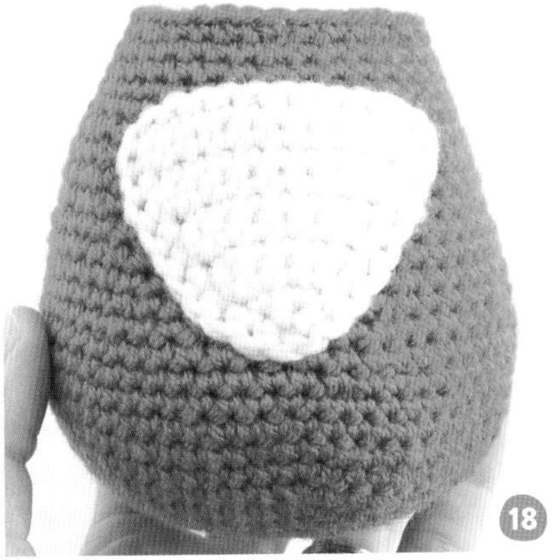
18

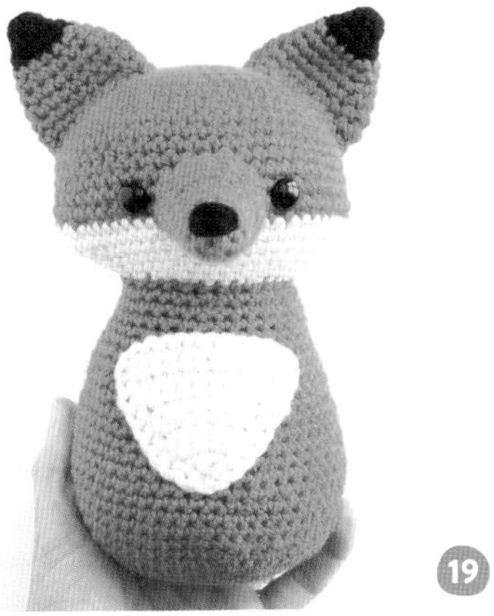
19

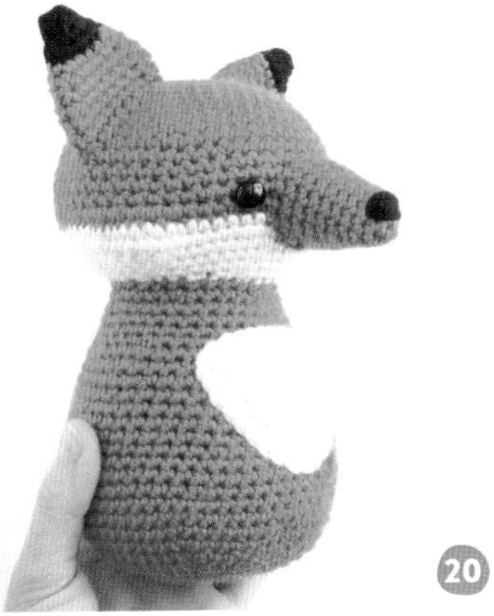
20

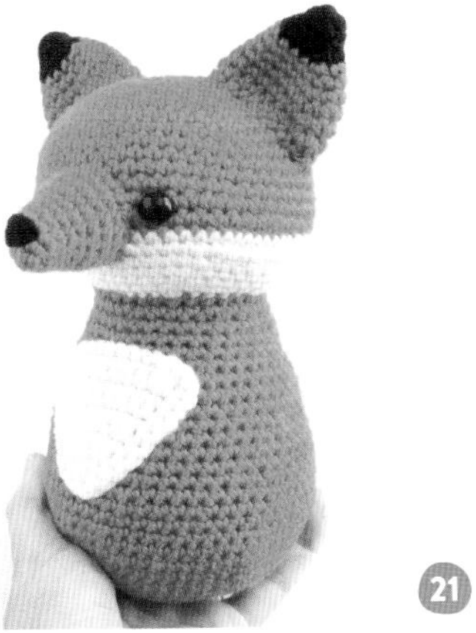
21

FRONT LEGS: MAKE 2

Using black yarn,

R1	6 sc in magic ring. (6 sts)
R2	Inc in each st around. (12 sts)
R3	*Sc 1, inc* 6 times. (18 sts)
R4	*Sc 2, inc* 6 times. (24 sts)
R5+6	Sc 24.
R7	Sc 6, inv dec 6 times, sc 6. (18 sts)
R8	Sc 6, inv dec 3 times, sc 6. (15 sts)
R9-12	Sc 15.

Begin adding fiberfill and continue adding as you work the piece.

Change to orange yarn,

R13	Sc 15, alternating between orange and black yarn for every other stitch. Simply make one sc in orange, then make one sc in black, repeating until you reach the end. (photos 22-25) The triangle shape will automatically form. The round will end with orange. Fasten off the black yarn. (photo 26)
R14-20	Sc 15. (photo 27)
R21	Sc 7. Next line up the stitches on both sides of the leg, then insert the hook into both stitches. Sc across 7 times. This will ensure the toes are pointing out once sewn to body. (photos 28-31)

Fasten off and leave a tail for sewing. (photo 32)

Using straight pins, pin the legs to the front of the body near round 27. The front legs will go above the chest piece. With the yarn needle and the tail, sew the legs to the body. Weave the needle under both loops (the "V") from R21 of the legs and then into the body. (photos 33+34) Repeat until you reach the end. Secure with a knot and hide inside the body. (photos 35-37)

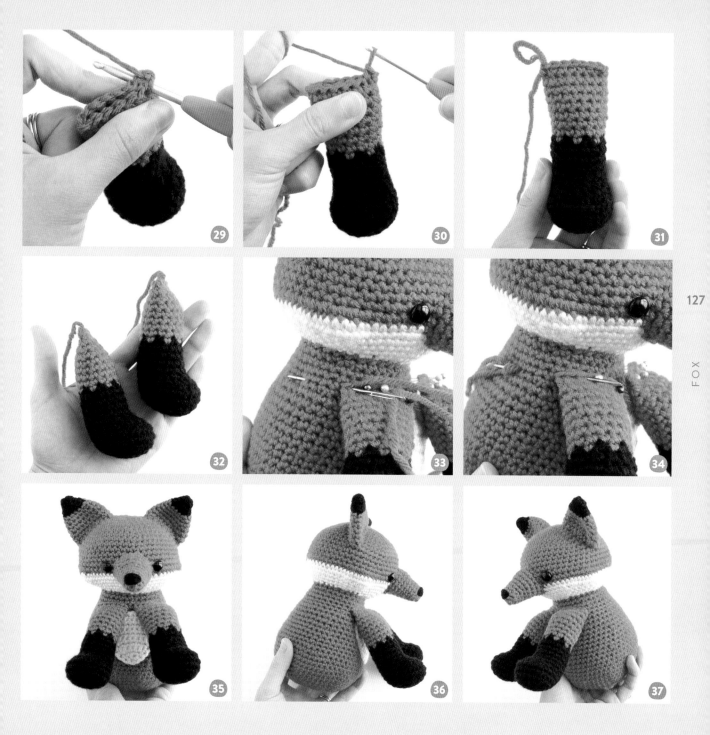

BACK LEGS: MAKE 2

Using black yarn,

R1	6 sc in magic ring. (6 sts)
R2	Inc in each st around. (12 sts)
R3	*Sc 1, inc* 6 times. (18 sts)
R4	*Sc 2, inc* 6 times. (24 sts)
R5+6	Sc 24.
R7	Sc 6, inv dec 6 times, sc 6. (18 sts)
R8	Sc 6, inv dec 3 times, sc 6. (15 sts)
R9-12	Sc 15.

Begin adding fiberfill and continue adding as you work the piece.

Change to orange yarn,

R13 Sc 15, alternating between orange and black yarn for every other stitch. Simply make one sc in orange, then make one sc in black, repeating until you reach the end. The triangle shape will automatically form. The round will end with orange. Fasten off the black yarn. *Refer to photos 22-27 of the front legs for guidance.*

R14-20 Sc 15.

R21 Sc 2. Next line up the stitches on both sides of the leg, then insert the hook into both stitches. Sc across 7 times. This will ensure the toes are pointing up once sewn to body. (photos 38-41)

Fasten off and leave a tail for sewing. (photo 42)

Using straight pins, pin the legs to the side of the body between rounds 9-16. With the yarn needle and the tail, sew the legs to the body. Weave the needle under both loops (the "V") from R21 of the legs and then into the body. (photo 43) Repeat until you reach the end.

With the same yarn tail, sew the upper legs to the body. This helps keep the legs closer instead of them being outstretched. Weave the needle through the upper and inner part of the leg and then into the body.

Pull the needle through one of the stitch holes on the body. Then insert into the same stitch hole and weave through to the leg. Repeat until you've sewn across the entire upper leg. Secure with a knot and hide inside the body. (photos 44-47)

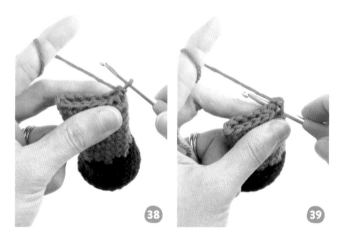

TAIL

Using cream yarn,

R1	6 sc in magic ring. (6 sts)
R2	*Sc 1, inc* 3 times. (9 sts)
R3	Sc 9.
R4	*Sc 2, inc* 3 times. (12 sts)
R5	*Sc 1, inc* 6 times. (18 sts)
R6	Sc 18.
R7	*Sc 2, inc* 6 times. (24 sts)
R8	*Sc 3, inc* 6 times. (30 sts)

Change to orange yarn,

R9	Sc 30, alternating between orange and cream yarn every two stitches. Simply make two sc in orange, then make two sc in cream, repeating until you reach the end. (photos 48-50) The triangle shape will automatically form. The round will end with orange. Fasten off the cream yarn.
R10-13	Sc 30. (photo 51)
R14	*Sc 8, inv dec* 3 times. (27 sts)
R15+16	Sc 27.
R17	*Sc 7, inv dec* 3 times. (24 sts)
R18+19	Sc 24.

Begin adding fiberfill and continue adding as you work the piece.

R20	*Sc 6, inv dec* 3 times. (21 sts)
R21+22	Sc 21.
R23	*Sc 5, inv dec* 3 times. (18 sts)
R24+25	Sc 18.
R26	*Sc 4, inv dec* 3 times. (15 sts)
R27+28	Sc 15.

Fasten off and leave a tail for sewing. (photo 52)

Using straight pins, pin the tail to the back of the body between rounds 9-13. (photo 53) Pin the tail at a slight angle so it can be seen from the front. With the yarn needle and the tail, sew the tail to the body. If sewing at an angle, make sure to sew some of the side of the tail to the body so it stays in place. Secure with a knot and hide inside the body. (photos 54-57)

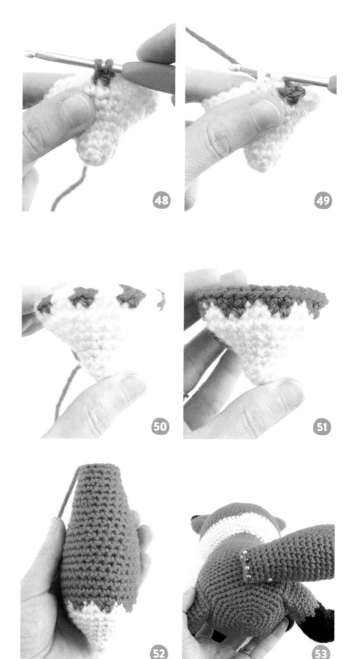

OWL

BEGINNER

 FINISHED MEASUREMENTS
- Approx. 6 inches wide by 5.5 inches tall

 MATERIALS
- Worsted weight yarn: Brown, Tan, and Mustard Yellow
- Size F/3.75mm crochet hook
- One pair of 12mm safety eyes
- Polyester fiberfill stuffing
- Yarn needle
- Scissors
- Stitch marker
- Straight pins

 ABBREVIATIONS
- Ch- Chain
- Dc- Double Crochet
- Hdc- Half Double Crochet
- Hdc Inc- Half Double Crochet Increase
- Inc- Increase
- Inv Dec- Invisible Decrease
- R- Round/Row
- Sc- Single Crochet
- St/s- Stitch/es

BODY

Using brown yarn,

R1	6 sc in magic ring. (6 sts)
R2	Inc in each st around. (12 sts)
R3	*Sc 1, inc* 6 times. (18 sts)
R4	*Sc 2, inc* 6 times. (24 sts)
R5	*Sc 3, inc* 6 times. (30 sts)
R6	*Sc 4, inc* 6 times. (36 sts)
R7	*Sc 5, inc* 6 times. (42 sts)
R8	*Sc 6, inc* 6 times. (48 sts)
R9	*Sc 7, inc* 6 times. (54 sts)
R10	Sc 54.
R11	*Sc 8, inc* 6 times. (60 sts)
R12-19	Sc 60.
R20	*Sc 14, inc* 4 times. (64 sts)
R21	Sc 64.
R22	*Sc 15, inc* 4 times. (68 sts)
R23-29	Sc 68.
R30	*Sc 15, inv dec* 4 times. (64 sts)
R31	Sc 64.
R32	*Sc 14, inv dec* 4 times. (60 sts)
R33	Sc 60.
R34	*Sc 8, inv dec* 6 times. (54 sts)
R35	*Sc 7, inv dec* 6 times. (48 sts)
R36	*Sc 6, inv dec* 6 times. (42 sts)
R37	*Sc 5, inv dec* 6 times. (36 sts)

Begin adding fiberfill and continue adding as you close the piece.

R38	*Sc 4, inv dec* 6 times. (30 sts)
R39	*Sc 3, inv dec* 6 times. (24 sts)
R40	*Sc 2, inv dec* 6 times. (18 sts)
R41	*Sc 1, inv dec* 6 times. (12 sts)
R42	Inv dec around 6 times. (6 sts)

Fasten off and leave a tail to close the piece. (photo 1)

MAIN EYE CIRCLES: MAKE 2

Using tan yarn,

R1	6 sc in magic ring. (6 sts)
R2	Inc in each st around. (12 sts)
R3	*Sc 1, inc* 6 times. (18 sts)
R4	Ch 1, hdc, hdc inc, *hdc in the next two sts, hdc inc* 5 times, hdc. (24 sts)

Fasten off and leave a tail for sewing. Weave in the starting tail. (photo 2)

COLORED EYE CIRCLES: MAKE 2

Using mustard yellow yarn,

R1	6 sc in magic ring. (6 sts)
R2	Inc in each st around. (12 sts)

Fasten off and leave a tail for sewing. Weave in the starting tail. (photo 3)

Use a chopstick or the end of a crochet hook to open the center of the magic ring up a little bit. This will help with getting the safety eyes inserted. (photos 4+5) With the safety eyes, insert into the center of the magic rings on each yellow circle, followed by the tan circles. (photo 6) Attach the safety backings to the eyes. With the yarn needle and the yellow tail, sew the circle to the tan circle. Weave the needle under both loops (the "V") from the stitches in R2 of the yellow circle and then through the tan circle. When coming back to the front of the work, weave the needle into the next stitch and pull through. (photos 7-9) Sew all the way around then secure the yellow tail with a knot.

Then, using straight pins, pin the eye circles to the body between rounds 12-22. (photo 10) With the yarn needle and the tail, sew the circles into place on the body. Weave the needle under both loops (the "V") from the stitches on R4 of the tan circle and then into the body, coming out through one of the stitch holes. Insert the needle into the same stitch hole and then go over to the next stitch on the eye piece and repeat. (photos 11+12) Make sure to go under the stitches and not over them to create a clean finish. Secure with a knot and hide inside the body. (photo 13)

BEAK

Using mustard yellow yarn,

R1 Ch 5 then starting in the 2nd ch from hook, sc, hdc, dc, hdc. (4 sts) (photos 14+15)

Fasten off and leave a tail for sewing.

Using straight pins, pin the beak in between the eye circles near round 15. With the yarn needle and the tail, sew the beak in place on the body. Sew across the part near the last hdc, then tack the tip of the beak down. Secure both tails with a knot and hide inside the body. (photo 16)

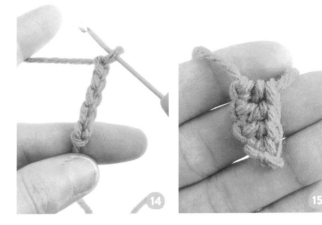

WINGS: MAKE 2

Using brown yarn,

R1	6 sc in magic ring. (6 sts)
R2	Inc in each st around. (12 sts)
R3	Sc 12.
R4	*Sc 1, inc* 6 times. (18 sts)
R5	Sc 18.
R6	*Sc 2, inc * 6 times. (24 sts)
R7-10	Sc 24.
R11	*Sc 2, inv dec* 6 times. (18 sts)
R12	Sc 18.
R13	*Sc 1, inv dec* 6 times. (12 sts)
R14	Sc 5. Do this by lining up the stitches on both sides of the wing, then inserting the hook into both stitches. Then sc as normal. (photos 17-20)

Fasten off and leave a tail for sewing. Leave wings unstuffed. (photo 21)

Using straight pins, pin the wings to the sides of the body near round 19. With the yarn needle and the tail, sew the wings to the body. Weave the needle under both loops (the "V") from R14 of the wings and then into the body. (photo 22) Secure with a knot and hide inside the body. (photos 23-25)

HAIR

With brown yarn, cut 4 strands, each about 5 inches long. With the crochet hook, insert the hook under round 8 and loop two yarn strands over the hook. (photos 26+27) Pull the hook through, bringing the two strands with it. (photo 28) Don't pull all the way through! Next, take the loose strands and pull them through the loop. (photo 29) Pull gently to tighten and then trim the strands to about 1 inch. (photo 30) Repeat on the other side of the body. (photos 31+32)

FEATHER DETAILING

Using straight pins, mark out where you would like to stitch each V. For mine, I used all one color for each V to make it easier for knowing where to insert the yarn needle. Space each pin 2 stitches apart, then add the bottom pin in the center of those two, about 2 rounds down.

The first row will be between R26+27 and there will be 3 V's.

The second row will be between R29+30 and there will be 4 V's.

The third row will be between R32+33 and there will be 3 V's.

Make sure to off center each row of V's. (photo 33)

Cut a long length of tan yarn and tie a knot at one end. Weave the needle through one of the stitch holes on the side of the body and come to your first pin on the side. Remove the pin and weave the needle through the stitch hole, pulling the yarn through. (photo 34) Remove the bottom pin and insert the yarn needle into the stitch hole. (photo 35) Remove the third pin of that color and weave the needle through the stitch hole. Come back down to the bottom stitch hole and insert the needle again. Weave the needle over to the next set of colored pins (or the next V), and then pull the yarn through to complete the first V. (photos 36+37) Repeat for all the V's. Secure with a knot and hide inside the body. (photos 38-40)

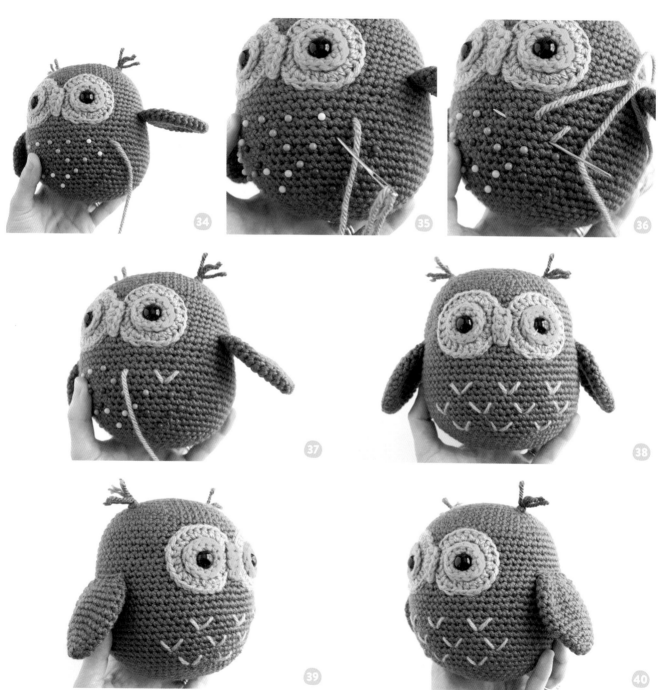

RACCOON

INTERMEDIATE

FINISHED MEASUREMENTS
- ✂ Approx. 6.5 inches wide by 7.5 inches tall by 9 inches long

MATERIALS
- ✂ Worsted weight yarn: White, Light Gray, Dark Gray, and Black
- ✂ Size F/3.75mm crochet hook
- ✂ One pair of 10.5mm safety eyes
- ✂ Polyester fiberfill stuffing
- ✂ Yarn needle
- ✂ Scissors
- ✂ Stitch marker
- ✂ Straight pins
- ✂ Optional: Hot glue gun

ABBREVIATIONS
- ✂ Ch- Chain
- ✂ Dc- Double Crochet
- ✂ Dc Inc- Double Crochet Increase
- ✂ Dec- Decrease
- ✂ Hdc- Half Double Crochet
- ✂ Hdc Inc- Half Double Crochet Increase
- ✂ Inc- Increase
- ✂ Inv Dec- Invisible Decrease
- ✂ R- Round/Row
- ✂ Sc- Single Crochet
- ✂ St/s- Stitch/es

EYE PATCHES: MAKE 2

Using dark gray yarn,

R1	Ch 9 then starting in the 2nd ch from hook and in both loops leaving the back "bump", sc in each chain across 8 times. Turn and then sc across the back "bumps", 8 times. (16 sts) (photos 1-5)
R2	Inc, sc 6, inc in the next two sts, sc 6, inc. (20 sts)
R3	Inc in the next two sts, sc 7, inc in the next three sts, sc 7, inc. (26 sts)

Fasten off and leave a tail for sewing. (photo 6)
Place a safety eye between rows 1 and 2 on each eye patch. Do not attach the safety backings yet. Set eye patches aside. (photo 7)

HEAD

Using light gray yarn,

R1	6 sc in magic ring. (6 sts)
R2	Inc in each st around. (12 sts)
R3	*Sc 1, inc* 6 times. (18 sts)
R4	*Sc 2, inc* 6 times. (24 sts)
R5	*Sc 3, inc* 6 times. (30 sts)
R6	*Sc 4, inc* 6 times. (36 sts)
R7	*Sc 5, inc* 6 times. (42 sts)
R8	*Sc 6, inc* 6 times. (48 sts)
R9	*Sc 7, inc* 6 times. (54 sts)
R10-15	Sc 54.
R16	*Sc 8, inc* 6 times. (60 sts)
R17	*Sc 9, inc* 6 times. (66 sts)
R18	*Sc 9, inv dec* 6 times. (60 sts)
R19	*Sc 8, inv dec* 6 times. (54 sts)
R20	*Sc 7, inv dec* 6 times. (48 sts)
R21	*Sc 6, inv dec* 6 times. (42 sts)

Add the safety eyes between rounds 14 and 15, placing them 7 stitches apart. The eye patches should sit between rounds 10-18 and should be about 2 stitches apart. Add the safety backings to the safety eyes. If it's too thick, try flipping the washer and attaching it backwards to the eye post. (photo 8)

With the yarn needle and the tail, sew the eye patches in place on the head. Make sure to sew them at a slight angle. Weave the needle under both loops (the "V") from the stitches on R3 of the eye patch and then into the head. To bring the needle back up, insert into the next stitch on the eye patch and pull through. (photos 9+10) Repeat until you reach the end. Make sure to go under the stitches and not over them to create a clean finish. Secure with a knot and trim tail.

R22	*Sc 5, inv dec* 6 times. (36 sts)

Begin adding fiberfill and continue adding as you close the piece.

R23	*Sc 4, inv dec* 6 times. (30 sts)
R24	*Sc 3, inv dec* 6 times. (24 sts)
R25	*Sc 2, inv dec* 6 times. (18 sts)
R26	*Sc 1, inv dec* 6 times. (12 sts)
R27	Inv dec around 6 times. (6 sts)

Fasten off and leave a tail to close the piece. (photos 11+12)

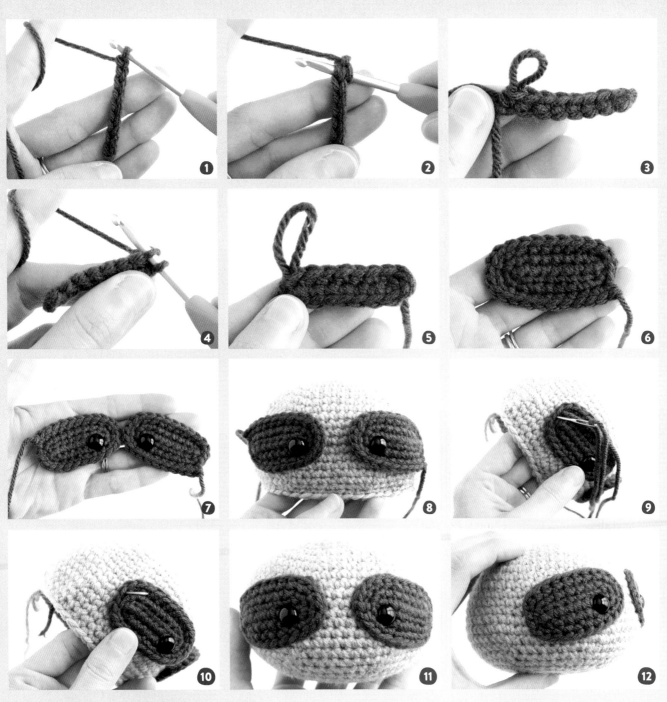

143

RACCOON

NOSE

Using white yarn,

R1	6 sc in magic ring. (6 sts)
R2	*Sc 1, inc* 3 times. (9 sts)
R3	*Sc 2, inc* 3 times. (12 sts)
R4	Sc 12.
R5	*Sc 3, inc* 3 times. (15 sts)
R6	Sc 15.

Fasten off and leave a tail for sewing. (photo 13)

TIP OF NOSE

Using black yarn,

R1	4 sc in magic ring. (4 sts)
R2	Inc in each st around. (8 sts)

Fasten off and leave a tail for sewing. (photo 14)

With the yarn needle and the tail, sew the black piece to the tip of the white nose. The black tip will sit over rounds 1 and 2 of the nose. Weave the needle under both loops (the "V") from the stitches on R3 of the tip and then into the nose. (photo 15) To bring the needle back up, insert into the next stitch on the tip and pull through. Repeat until you reach the end. Make sure to go under the stitches and not over them to create a clean finish. Secure with a knot and trim tail. (photo 16)

Add fiberfill to the nose. Using straight pins, pin the nose in between rounds 13 and 17. The nose will sit right in between and slightly on top of the eye patches. With the yarn needle and the tail, sew the nose to the head. Secure with a knot and hide inside the head. (photos 17+18)

144

RACCOON

WHITE STRIPS FOR EYES: MAKE 2

Using white yarn,

R1 Ch 19 then turn the chain over and work in the back bumps of the chain. Starting in the 2nd bump from hook, sc in each bump across. (18 sts) (photos 19-21)

Fasten off and leave a tail for sewing. (photo 22)

Using straight pins, pin the strips above both eye patches. Start where the top of the nose hits round 13 and go all the way around the eye patch to round 17 on the head. (photos 23-25)

With the yarn needle and the tail, sew the strips to the head. Weave the needle under both loops (the "V") from the stitches on R1 of the strip and then into the head, coming out through one of the stitch holes. Insert the needle into the same stitch hole and then go over to the next stitch on the strip and repeat. Make sure to go under the stitches and not over them to create a clean finish. Secure with a knot and hide inside the head.

Alternatively, you can use hot glue to secure these pieces down instead of sewing. Just make sure to secure the tails and hide inside the head.

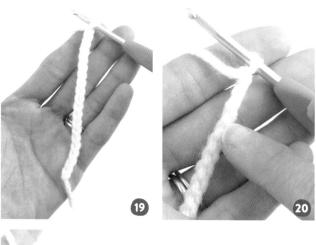

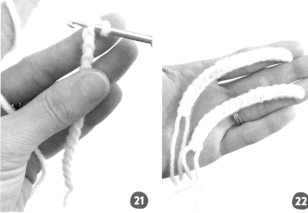

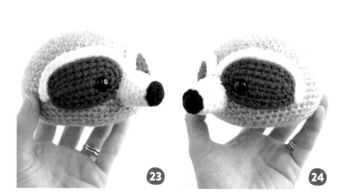

EARS: MAKE 2

Using light gray yarn,

R1	6 sc in magic ring. (6 sts)
R2	*Sc 1, inc* 3 times. (9 sts)
R3	*Sc 2, inc* 3 times. (12 sts)
R4	*Sc 3, inc* 3 times. (15 sts)
R5	*Sc 4, inc* 3 times. (18 sts)
R6	*Sc 5, inc* 3 times. (21 sts)
R7	*Sc 6, inc* 3 times. (24 sts)
R8	Sc 24.

Fasten off and leave a tail for sewing. Leave ears unstuffed. (photo 26)

Using straight pins, pin the ears to the head between rounds 5-15. With the yarn needle and the tail, sew the ears in place. Secure with a knot and hide inside the head. (photos 27-29)

INSIDE OF EAR: MAKE 2

Using dark gray yarn,

R1	Ch 7 then starting in the 2nd ch from hook and in both loops leaving the back "bump", sc in each chain across. (6 sts) Ch 1 and turn. (photos 30-32)
R2	Dec, sc 2, dec. (4 sts) Ch 1 and turn.
R3	Dec 2 times. (2 sts) Ch 1 and turn.
R4	Dec 1 time. (1 sts)

Fasten off and leave a tail for sewing. Weave in the starting tail. (photo 33)

Using straight pins, pin the inside pieces to the ears. (photo 34) With the yarn needle and the tail, sew the inside pieces to the ears. Weave the needle into the edge of the inside piece then into the ear. Pull the needle through both layers of the main ear and come out the back side. (photos 35+36) Insert the needle into the same stitch hole, weaving through to the front, then through the edge of the inside piece. (photos 37+38) This technique makes it so the stitching does not show on the back of the ear. Continue all the way around until you reach the end. Secure with a knot and hide inside the head. (photos 39+40)

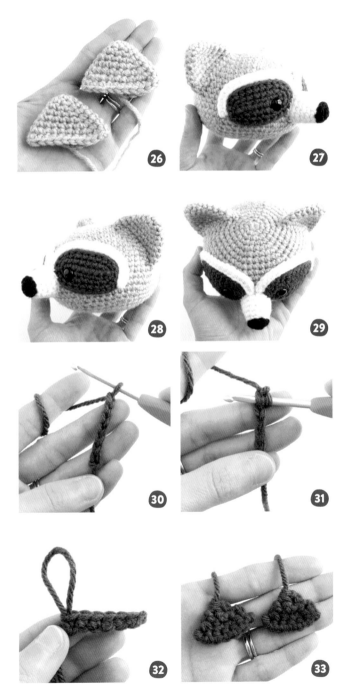

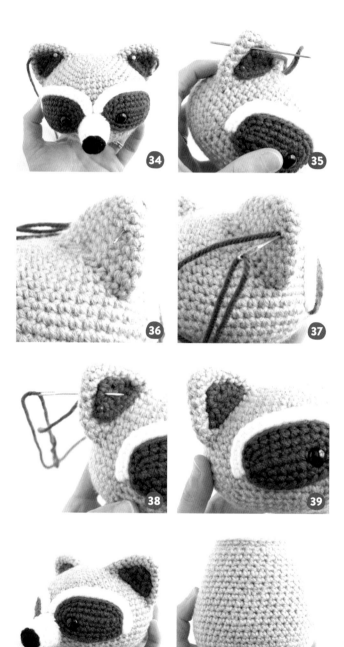

BODY

Using light gray yarn.

R1	6 sc in magic ring. (6 sts)
R2	Inc in each st around. (12 sts)
R3	*Sc 1, inc* 6 times. (18 sts)
R4	*Sc 2, inc* 6 times. (24 sts)
R5	*Sc 3, inc* 6 times. (30 sts)
R6	*Sc 4, inc* 6 times. (36 sts)
R7	*Sc 5, inc* 6 times. (42 sts)
R8	*Sc 6, inc* 6 times. (48 sts)
R9	*Sc 7, inc* 6 times. (54 sts)
R10	*Sc 8, inc* 6 times. (60 sts)
R11+12	Sc 60.
R13	*Sc 8, inv dec* 6 times. (54 sts)
R14-16	Sc 54.
R17	*Sc 7, inv dec* 6 times. (48 sts)
R18-20	Sc 48.
R21	*Sc 6, inv dec* 6 times. (42 sts)
R22-24	Sc 42.

Begin adding fiberfill and continue adding as you work the piece.

R25	*Sc 5, inv dec* 6 times. (36 sts)
R26-28	Sc 36.
R29	*Sc 4, inv dec* 6 times. (30 sts)
R30	Sc 30.

Fasten off and leave a long tail for sewing. (photo 41)

Using straight pins, pin the body to the head. With the yarn needle and the tail, sew the head in place on the body. If needed, add any extra fiberfill to the body before closing the piece. Secure with a knot and hide inside the body. (photo 42)

BELLY

Using white yarn,

R1	6 sc in magic ring. (6 sts)
R2	Inc in each st around. (12 sts)
R3	*Sc 1, inc* 6 times. (18 sts)
R4	Sc 1, inc, *Sc 2, inc* 5 times, sc 1. (24 sts)
R5	*Sc 3, inc* 6 times. (30 sts)
R6	Sc 2, inc, *Sc 4, inc* 5 times, sc 2. (36 sts)
R7	*Sc 5, inc* 6 times. (42 sts)
R8	Sc 16, sc hdc in one st, hdc inc, hdc dc in one st, dc inc, dc inc, dc inc, dc inc, dc hdc in one st, hdc inc, hdc sc in one st, sc 16. (52 sts)

Fasten off and leave a long tail for sewing. (photo 43)

Using straight pins, pin the belly to the body between rounds 10-29. With the yarn needle and the tail, sew the circle to the body. Weave the needle under both loops (the "V") from the stitches on R8 of the belly and then into the body, coming out through one of the stitch holes. Insert the needle into the same stitch hole and then go over to the next stitch on the belly and repeat. (photos 44+45) Make sure to go under the stitches and not over them to create a clean finish. Secure with a knot and hide inside the body. (photos 46+47)

ARMS: MAKE 2

Using dark gray yarn,

R1	6 sc in magic ring. (6 sts)
R2	Inc in each st around. (12 sts)
R3	*Sc 1, inc* 6 times. (18 sts)
R4+5	Sc 18.

Change to light gray yarn,

R6+7	Sc 18.
R8	*Sc 4, inv dec* 3 times. (15 sts)

Begin adding fiberfill and continue adding as you work the piece.

R9-17	Sc 15.
R18	Sc 7. Do this by lining up the stitches on both sides of the arm, then inserting the hook into both stitches. Then sc as normal. (photos 48-51)

Fasten off and leave a tail for sewing. (photo 52)

Using straight pins, pin the arms to the sides of the body between rounds 19-26. Make sure to pin the arms at a slight angle. With the yarn needle and the tail, sew the arms to the body. Weave the needle under both loops (the "V") from R18 of the arms and then into the body. (photos 53+54) Secure with a knot and hide inside the body. (photos 55-57)

43

44

45

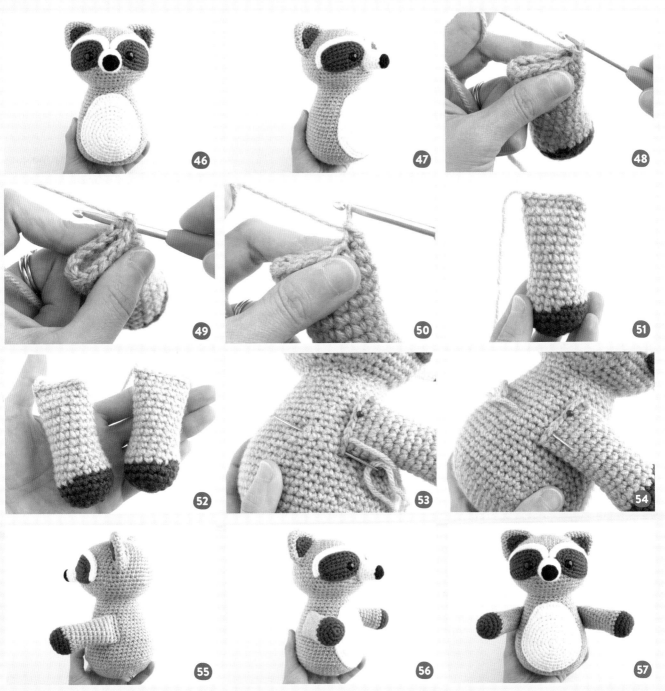

LEGS: MAKE 2

Using dark gray yarn,

R1	6 sc in magic ring. (6 sts)
R2	Inc in each st around. (12 sts)
R3	*Sc 1, inc* 6 times. (18 sts)
R4	*Sc 2, inc* 6 times. (24 sts)
R5	Sc 24.
R6	Sc 6, inv dec 6 times, sc 6. (18 sts)
R7	Sc 6, inv dec 3 times, sc 6. (15 sts)

Change to light gray yarn,

Begin adding fiberfill and continue adding as you work the piece.

R8-20	Sc 15.

Fasten off and leave a tail for sewing. (photo 58)

Using straight pins, pin the legs to the sides of the body between rounds 9-15. With the yarn needle and the tail, sew the legs to the body. Weave the needle under both loops (the "V") from R20 of the legs and then into the body. (photo 59)

With the same yarn tail, sew the upper legs to the body. This helps keep the legs closer instead of outstretched. Weave the needle through the upper and inner part of the leg and then into the body. Pull the needle through one of the stitch holes on the body. Then insert into the same stitch hole and weave through to the leg. Repeat until you've sewn across the entire upper leg. Secure with a knot and hide inside the body. (photos 60-62) *Check out the Sloth pattern for more in-depth photos on this step.*

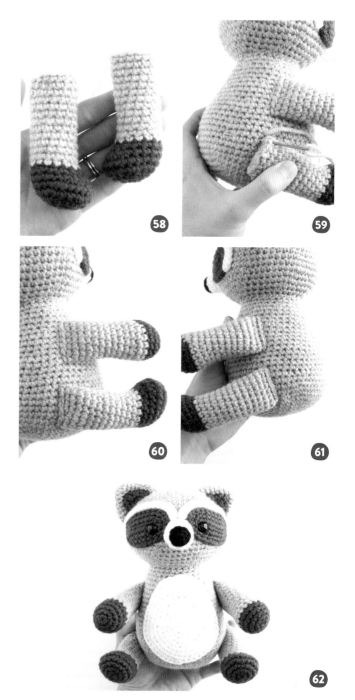

63

TAIL

Note: There are several color changes for this part of the pattern. When changing colors, simply drop the old color, pick up the new color, and continue crocheting as normal. This pattern is written so that when there is a color change, all you have to do is carry the yarn up the couple of rounds where it was last dropped.

Using dark gray yarn,

R1	6 sc in magic ring. (6 sts)
R2	Inc in each st around. (12 sts)
R3	Sc 12.
R4	*Sc 1, inc* 6 times. (18 sts)
R5	Sc 18.

Change to light gray yarn,

R6	*Sc 2, inc* 6 times. (24 sts)
R7+8	Sc 24.

Change to dark gray yarn,

R9+10	Sc 24.

Change to light gray yarn,

R11-13	Sc 24.

Change to dark gray yarn,

R14+15	Sc 24.

Change to light gray yarn,

R16	Sc 24.

Begin adding fiberfill and continue adding as you work the piece.

R17	*Sc 2, inv dec* 6 times. (18 sts)
R18	Sc 18.

Change to dark gray yarn,

R19+20	Sc 18.

Change to light gray yarn,

R21+22	Sc 18.

Fasten off and leave a tail for sewing. (photo 63)

Using straight pins, pin the tail to the body between rounds 9 and 14. With the yarn needle and the tail, sew the tail to the body. Secure with a knot and hide inside the body. (photos 64+65)

64

65

SKUNK

INTERMEDIATE

FINISHED MEASUREMENTS
- Approx. 6.5 inches wide by 7.5 inches tall by 7.5 inches long

MATERIALS
- Worsted weight yarn: Black, White, and Pink
- Size F/3.75mm crochet hook
- One pair of 10.5mm safety eyes
- Polyester fiberfill stuffing
- Yarn needle
- Scissors
- Stitch marker
- Straight pins
- Optional- Hot glue gun

ABBREVIATIONS
- Ch- Chain
- Dec- Decrease
- Hdc- Half Double Crochet
- Inc- Increase
- Inv Dec- Invisible Decrease
- R- Round/Row
- Sc- Single Crochet
- St/s- Stitch/es

HEAD

Using black yarn,

R1	6 sc in magic ring. (6 sts)
R2	Inc in each st around. (12 sts)
R3	*Sc 1, inc* 6 times. (18 sts)
R4	*Sc 2, inc* 6 times. (24 sts)
R5	*Sc 3, inc* 6 times. (30 sts)
R6	*Sc 4, inc* 6 times. (36 sts)
R7	*Sc 5, inc* 6 times. (42 sts)
R8	*Sc 6, inc* 6 times. (48 sts)
R9	*Sc 7, inc* 6 times. (54 sts)
R10-17	Sc 54.

Add the safety eyes between rounds 14 and 15, placing them about 8 stitches apart. With white yarn, stitch around the outside of the eyes. (photos 1+2)

R18	*Sc 8, inc* 6 times. (60 sts)
R19	Sc 60.
R20	*Sc 8, inv dec* 6 times. (54 sts)
R21	*Sc 7, inv dec* 6 times. (48 sts)
R22	*Sc 6, inv dec* 6 times. (42 sts)
R23	*Sc 5, inv dec* 6 times. (36 sts)

Begin adding fiberfill and continue adding as you close the piece.

R24	*Sc 4, inv dec* 6 times. (30 sts)
R25	*Sc 3, inv dec* 6 times. (24 sts)
R26	*Sc 2, inv dec* 6 times. (18 sts)
R27	*Sc 1, inv dec* 6 times. (12 sts)
R28	Inv dec around 6 times. (6 sts)

Fasten off and leave a tail to close the piece. (photo 3)

NOSE

Using black yarn,

R1	6 sc in magic ring. (6 sts)
R2	*Sc 1, inc* 3 times. (9 sts)
R3	*Sc 2, inc* 3 times. (12 sts)
R4	Sc 12.

Fasten off and leave a tail for sewing. (photo 4)

With pink yarn, sew a nose over the magic ring on the main nose piece. (photo 5) Go over the spot about 6 times to build up the nose. Secure with a knot and trim the end. Add fiberfill to the nose. Then, using straight pins, pin the nose to the head between rounds 13-18. With the yarn needle and the tail, sew the nose to the head. Secure with a knot and hide inside the head. (photos 6+7)

EARS: MAKE 2

Using black yarn,

R1	6 sc in magic ring. (6 sts)
R2	Inc in each st around. (12 sts)
R3	*Sc 1, inc* 6 times. (18 sts)
R4+5	Sc 18.
R6	*Sc 1, inv dec* 6 times. (12 sts)

Fasten off and leave a tail for sewing. Leave ears unstuffed. (photo 8)

Using straight pins, pin the ears to the head between rounds 7-12. With the yarn needle and the tail, sew the ears in place. Secure with a knot and hide inside the head. (photos 9-12)

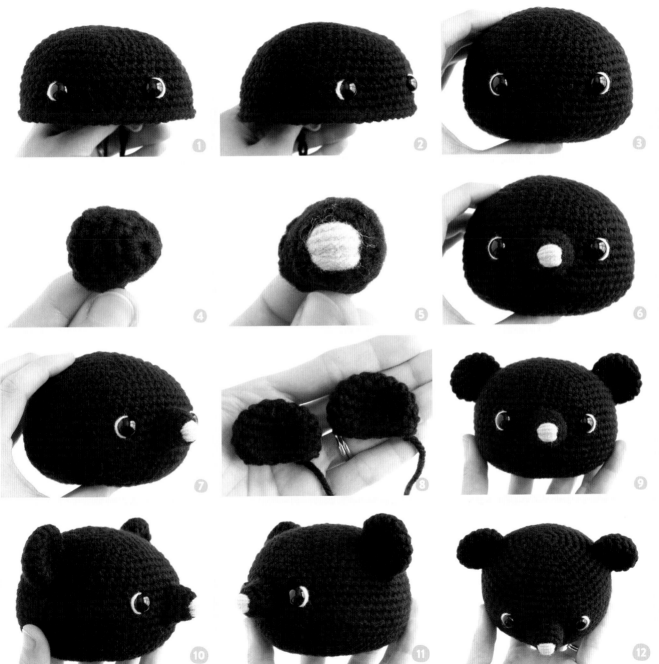

HAIR PIECE

Using white yarn,

R1 Ch 3 then starting in the 2nd ch from hook and in both loops leaving the back "bump", sc in each chain across. (2 sts) Ch 1 and turn. (photos 13+14)

R2 Inc in each stitch. (4 sts) Ch 1 and turn.

R3 Inc, sc 2, inc. (6 sts) Ch 1 and turn.

R4 Sc 6. Ch 1 and turn.

R5 Inc, sc 4, inc. (8 sts) Ch 1 and turn.

R6 Sc 8. Ch 1 and turn.

R7 Inc, sc 6, inc. (10 sts) Ch 1 and turn.

R8-31 Sc 10. Ch 1 and turn.

R32 Dec, sc 6, dec. (8 sts) Ch 1 and turn.

R33 Dec, sc 4, dec. (6 sts) Ch 1 and turn.

R34 Dec, sc 2, dec. (4 sts)

Fasten off and leave a long tail for sewing. Weave in the starting tail. (photo 15)

Using straight pins, pin the hair piece near round 12, right above the top of the nose. Go between the ears and down the back of the head until it reaches round 20. (photos 16-18) With the yarn needle and the tail, sew the hair piece in place. Weave the needle through the edge of the piece and then into the body, coming out through one of the stitch holes. (photo 19) Insert the needle into the same stitch hole and then go over to the next space along the edge and repeat. (photos 20+21) Secure with a knot and hide inside the head. (photos 22-25)

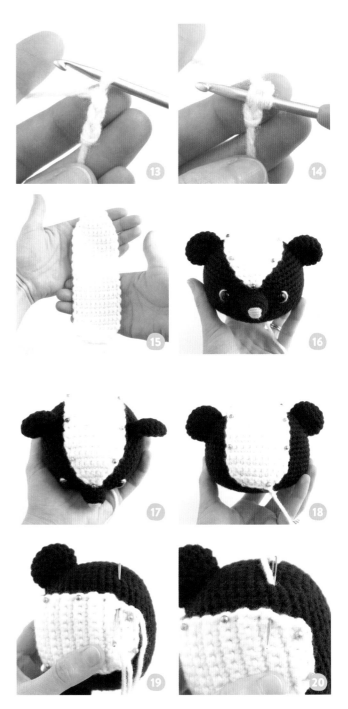

BODY

Using black yarn,

R1	6 sc in magic ring. (6 sts)
R2	Inc in each st around. (12 sts)
R3	*Sc 1, inc* 6 times. (18 sts)
R4	*Sc 2, inc* 6 times. (24 sts)
R5	*Sc 3, inc* 6 times. (30 sts)
R6	*Sc 4, inc* 6 times. (36 sts)
R7	*Sc 5, inc* 6 times. (42 sts)
R8	*Sc 6, inc* 6 times. (48 sts)
R9	*Sc 7, inc* 6 times. (54 sts)
R10	*Sc 8, inc* 6 times. (60 sts)
R11+12	Sc 60.
R13	*Sc 8, inv dec* 6 times. (54 sts)
R14+15	Sc 54.
R16	*Sc 7, inv dec* 6 times. (48 sts)
R17-19	Sc 48.
R20	*Sc 6, inv dec* 6 times. (42 sts)
R21-23	Sc 42.

Begin adding fiberfill and continue adding as you work the piece.

R24	*Sc 5, inv dec* 6 times. (36 sts)
R25+26	Sc 36.
R27	*Sc 4, inv dec* 6 times. (30 sts)
R28+29	Sc 30.

Fasten off and leave a tail for sewing. (photo 26)

Using straight pins, pin the body to the head. With the yarn needle and the tail, sew the head in place on the body. If needed, add any extra fiberfill to the body before closing the piece. Secure with a knot and hide inside the body. (photos 27+28)

BELLY

Using white yarn,

R1	6 sc in magic ring. (6 sts)
R2	Inc in each st around. (12 sts)
R3	*Sc 1, inc* 6 times. (18 sts)
R4	Sc 1, inc, *Sc 2, inc* 5 times, sc 1. (24 sts)
R5	*Sc 3, inc* 6 times. (30 sts)
R6	Sc 2, inc, *Sc 4, inc* 5 times, sc 2. (36 sts)
R7	*Sc 5, inc* 6 times. (42 sts)
R8	Sc 3, inc, *Sc 6, inc* 5 times, sc 3. (48 sts)

Fasten off and leave a long tail for sewing. (photo 29)

Using straight pins, pin the belly to the body between rounds 11-27. With the yarn needle and the tail, sew the circle to the body. Weave the needle under both loops (the "V") from the stitches on R8 of the belly and then into the body, coming out through one of the stitch holes. Insert the needle into the same stitch hole and then go over to the next stitch on the belly and repeat. (photos 30+31) Make sure to go under the stitches and not over them to create a clean finish. Secure with a knot and hide inside the body. (photos 32+33)

ARMS: MAKE 2

Using black yarn,

R1	6 sc in magic ring. (6 sts)
R2	Inc in each st around. (12 sts)
R3	*Sc 1, inc* 6 times. (18 sts)
R4+5	Sc 18.
R6	*Sc 4, inv dec* 3 times. (15 sts)
R7+8	Sc 15.
R9	*Sc 3, inv dec* 3 times. (12 sts)

Begin adding fiberfill and continue adding as you work the piece.

R10-15	Sc 12.
R16	Sc 5. Do this by lining up the stitches on both sides of the arm, then inserting the hook into both stitches. Then sc as normal. (photos 34-37)

Fasten off and leave a tail for sewing. (photo 38)

Using straight pins, pin the arms to the sides of the body between rounds 21-26. Make sure to pin the arms at a slight angle. With the yarn needle and the tail, sew the arms to the body. (photos 39+40) Weave the needle under both loops (the "V") from R16 of the arms and then into the body. Secure with a knot and hide inside the body. (photos 41+42)

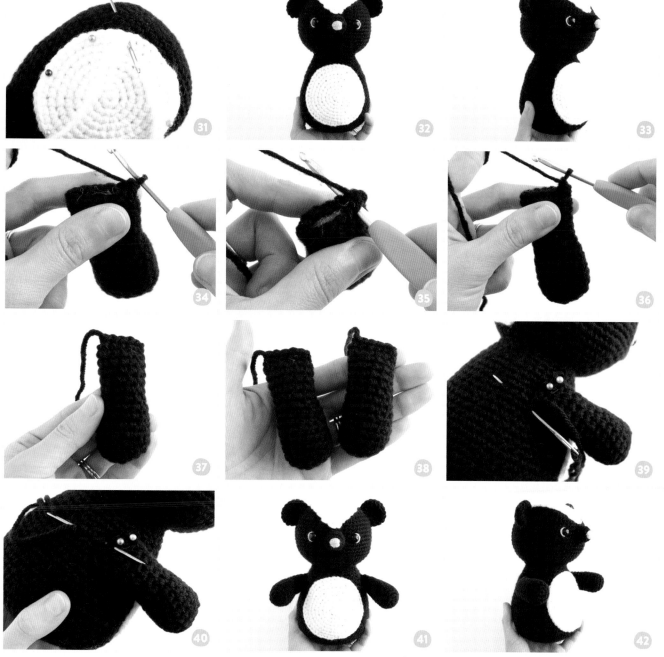

LEGS: MAKE 2

Using black yarn,

R1	6 sc in magic ring. (6 sts)
R2	Inc in each st around. (12 sts)
R3	Sc 3, inc in the next six sts, sc 3. (18 sts)
R4	Sc 6, inc in the next six sts, sc 6. (24 sts)
R5	Sc 24.
R6	Sc 6, inv dec 6 times, sc 6. (18 sts)
R7	Sc 6, inv dec 3 times, sc 6. (15 sts)

Begin adding fiberfill and continue adding as you work the piece.

R8-18	Sc 15.
R19	Sc 2. Next line up the stitches on both sides of the leg, then insert the hook into both stitches. Sc across 7 times. This will ensure the toes are pointing up once sewn to body. (photos 43-46)

Fasten off and leave a tail for sewing. (photo 47)

Using straight pins, pin the legs to the sides of the body between rounds 10-16. With the yarn needle and the tail, sew the legs to the body. Weave the needle under both loops (the "V") from R19 of the legs and then into the body. (photos 48+49) Secure with a knot and hide inside the body. (photos 50+51)

BACK STRIPES: MAKE 2

Using white yarn,

R1	Ch 16 then starting in the 2nd ch from hook and in both loops leaving the back "bump", hdc in each chain across. (15 sts) (photo 52)

Fasten off and leave a tail for sewing. (photo 53)

Using straight pins, pin the stripes to the body between rounds 12-28. Make sure to position them so they are curved. (photo 54) With the yarn needle and the tail, sew the stripes to the body. Weave the needle under both loops (the "V") from the stitches on R1 of the stripe and then into the body, coming

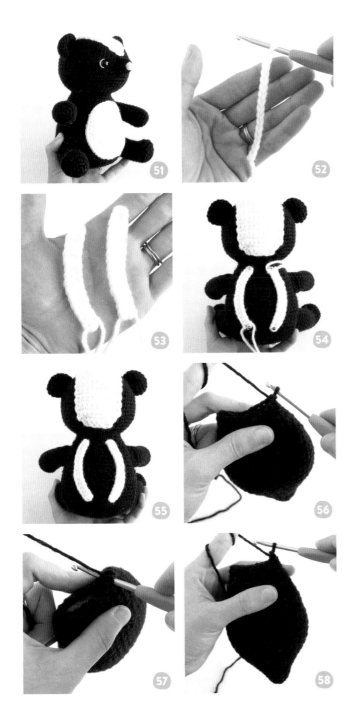

out through one of the stitch holes. Insert the needle into the same stitch hole and then go over to the next stitch on the stripe and repeat. Continue all the way around the piece. Make sure to go under the stitches and not over them to create a clean finish. Secure with a knot and hide inside the body. (photo 55)

Alternatively, you can use hot glue to secure these pieces down instead of sewing. Just make sure to secure the tails and hide inside the body.

TAIL

Using black yarn,

R1	6 sc in magic ring. (6 sts)
R2	*Sc 1, inc* 3 times. (9 sts)
R3	*Sc 2, inc* 3 times. (12 sts)
R4	Sc 12.
R5	*Sc 3, inc* 3 times. (15 sts)
R6	*Sc 4, inc* 3 times. (18 sts)
R7	*Sc 5, inc* 3 times. (21 sts)
R8	*Sc 6, inc* 3 times. (24 sts)
R9	*Sc 3, inc* 6 times. (30 sts)
R10	*Sc 4, inc* 6 times. (36 sts)
R11-15	Sc 36.
R16	*Sc 4, inv dec* 6 times. (30 sts)
R17+18	Sc 30.
R19	*Sc 3, inv dec* 6 times. (24 sts)

Begin adding fiberfill and continue adding as you work the piece.

R20-22	Sc 24.
R23	*Sc 2, inv dec* 6 times. (18 sts)
R24+25	Sc 18.
R26	Sc 8. Do this by lining up the stitches on both sides of the tail, then inserting the hook into both stitches. Then sc as normal. (photos 56-59)

Fasten off and leave a tail for sewing. Set aside. (photo 60)

TAIL STRIPE

Using white yarn,

R1   Ch 38 then starting in the 2nd ch from
hook and in both loops leaving the
back "bump", hdc in the next 18 spaces,
in the next space hdc ch 1 hdc, then
hdc in the remaining 18 spaces. (39 sts,
including the ch 1) (photos 61-63)

Fasten off and leave a tail for sewing. (photo 64)

Using straight pins, pin the stripe to the tail between
rounds 7-25. (photo 65) Make sure to place the stripe
so it goes along with the shape of the tail. With the
yarn needle and the tail, sew the stripe to the tail.
Weave the needle under both loops (the "V") from
the stitches on R1 of the stripe and then into the
body, coming out through one of the stitch holes.
Insert the needle into the same stitch hole and then
go over to the next stitch on the stripe and repeat.
Continue all the way around the piece. Make sure to
go under the stitches and not over them to create a
clean finish. Secure with a knot and hide inside the
tail. (photos 66+67)

Alternatively, use a hot glue gun to secure the stripe
in place.

Next, use straight pins to pin the tail to the back of
the body near round 11. (photo 68) With the yarn
needle and the tail, sew the tail to the body. Weave
the needle under both loops (the "V") from R26 of the
tail and then into the body. (photos 69+70) Secure
with a knot and hide inside the body. (photos 71-73)

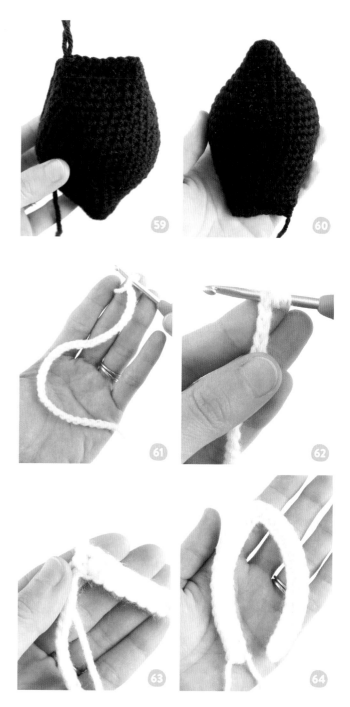

SQUIRREL

BEGINNER

FINISHED MEASUREMENTS
✂ Approx. 4.5 inches wide by 7 inches tall by 7 inches long

MATERIALS
✂ Worsted weight yarn: Light Brown, Cream, Dark Brown, and White
✂ Size F/3.75mm crochet hook
✂ One pair of 10.5mm safety eyes
✂ Polyester fiberfill stuffing
✂ Yarn needle
✂ Scissors
✂ Stitch marker
✂ Straight pins
✂ Optional: Pet slicker brush

ABBREVIATIONS
✂ Ch- Chain
✂ Dec- Decrease
✂ Inc- Increase
✂ Inv Dec- Invisible Decrease
✂ R- Round/Row
✂ Sc- Single Crochet
✂ St/s- Stitch/es

HEAD

Using light brown yarn,

R1	6 sc in magic ring. (6 sts)
R2	Sc 6.
R3	Inc in each st around. (12 sts)
R4	*Sc 1, inc* 6 times. (18 sts)
R5	*Sc 2, inc* 6 times. (24 sts)
R6	*Sc 3, inc* 6 times. (30 sts)
R7	Sc 30.

With dark brown yarn, stitch the nose over rounds 2 and 3, spanning 4 stitches in length. (photo 1) Go over the spot about 6 times to build up the nose. (photo 2) Then stitch one line down the center. (photo 3) Secure with a knot and hide inside the head.

R8	*Sc 4, inc* 6 times. (36 sts)
R9	*Sc 5, inc* 6 times. (42 sts)
R10-19	Sc 42. After round 11, add the safety eyes.

Add the safety eyes between rounds 8 and 9, placing them about 17 stitches apart. With white yarn, stitch around the outside of the eye. (photos 4-6)

R20	*Sc 5, inv dec* 6 times. (36 sts)
R21	Sc 36.

Begin adding fiberfill and continue adding as you close the piece.

R22	*Sc 4, inv dec* 6 times. (30 sts)
R23	*Sc 3, inv dec* 6 times. (24 sts)
R24	*Sc 2, inv dec* 6 times. (18 sts)
R25	*Sc 1, inv dec* 6 times. (12 sts)
R26	Inv dec around 6 times. (6 sts)

Fasten off and leave a tail to close the piece. (photo 7)

EARS: MAKE 2

Using light brown yarn,

R1	5 sc in magic ring. (5 sts)
R2	Inc in each st around. (10 sts)
R3	*Sc 1, inc* 5 times. (15 sts)

Fasten off and leave a tail for sewing. Weave in the starting tail. (photo 8)

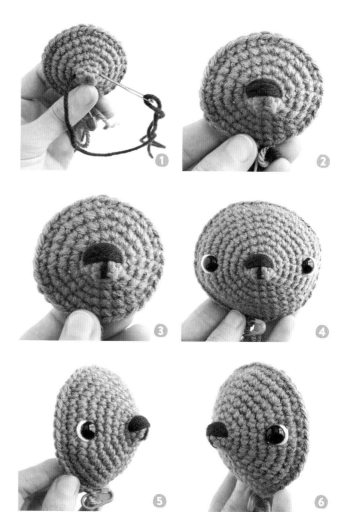

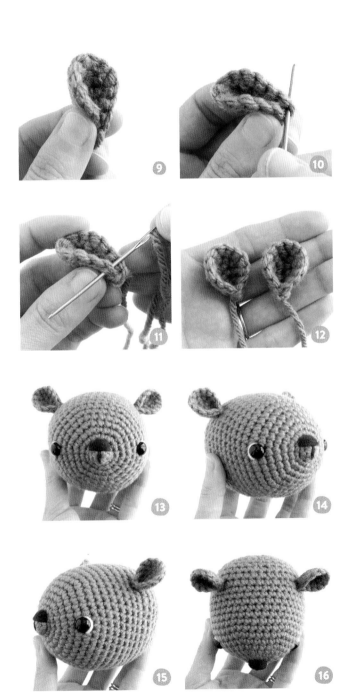

Pinch the bottom of round 3 together. (photo 9) With the yarn needle and the tail, sew the pinched area together. (photos 10-12) Using straight pins, pin the ears between rounds 17 and 18, placing them about 11 stitches apart. With the yarn needle and tail, sew the ears into place. Secure with a knot and hide inside the head. (photos 13-16)

BODY

Using light brown yarn,

R1	6 sc in magic ring. (6 sts)
R2	Inc in each st around. (12 sts)
R3	*Sc 1, inc* 6 times. (18 sts)
R4	*Sc 2, inc* 6 times. (24 sts)
R5	*Sc 3, inc* 6 times. (30 sts)
R6	*Sc 4, inc* 6 times. (36 sts)
R7	*Sc 5, inc* 6 times. (42 sts)
R8	*Sc 6, inc* 6 times. (48 sts)
R9	*Sc 7, inc* 6 times. (54 sts)
R10+11	Sc 54.
R12	*Sc 7, inv dec* 6 times. (48 sts)
R13+14	Sc 48.
R15	*Sc 6, inv dec* 6 times. (42 sts)
R16-18	Sc 42.

Begin adding fiberfill and continue adding as you work the piece.

R19	*Sc 5, inv dec* 6 times. (36 sts)
R20-22	Sc 36.
R23	*Sc 4, inv dec* 6 times. (30 sts)
R24+25	Sc 30.
R26	*Sc 3, inv dec* 6 times. (24 sts)
R27	Sc 24.

Fasten off and leave a long tail for sewing. (photo 17)

BELLY

Using cream yarn,

R1   Ch 7 then starting in the 2nd ch from hook and in both loops leaving the back "bump", sc in each chain across. (6 sts) Ch 1 and turn. (photos 18-20)

R2   Inc, sc 4, inc. (8 sts) Ch 1 and turn.

R3   Inc, sc 6, inc. (10 sts) Ch 1 and turn.

R4   Inc, sc 8, inc. (12 sts) Ch 1 and turn.

R5   Inc, sc 10, inc. (14 sts) Ch 1 and turn.

R6-8   Sc 14. Ch 1 and turn.

R9   Dec, sc 10, dec. (12 sts) Ch 1 and turn.

R10   Sc 12. Ch 1 and turn.

R11   Dec, sc 8, dec. (10 sts) Ch 1 and turn.

R12+13   Sc 10. Ch 1 and turn.

R14   Dec, sc 6, dec. (8 sts) Ch 1 and turn.

R15+16   Sc 8. Ch 1 and turn.

R17   Dec, sc 4, dec. (6 sts) Ch 1 and turn. (photo 21)

For this next row we are going to work around the edge of the belly.

R18   Sc in the same st as the last sc, then continue single crocheting all the way around the edge. Stop when you have reached the first stitch from R17. (44 sts) (photos 22+23)

Fasten off and leave an extra-long tail for sewing. Weave in the starting tail.

Using straight pins, pin the belly to the body between rounds 9-26. With the yarn needle and the tail, sew the belly to the body. Weave the needle under both loops (the "V") from the stitches on R18 of the belly and then into the body, coming out through one of the stitch holes. Insert the needle into the same stitch hole and then go over to the next stitch on the belly and repeat. Make sure to go under the stitches and not over them to create a clean finish. (photos 24+25) Secure with a knot and hide inside the body. (photo 26)

Using straight pins, pin the body to the head. With the yarn needle and the tail, sew the head in place on the body. If needed, add any extra fiberfill to the body before closing the piece. Secure with a knot and hide inside the body. (photos 27+28)

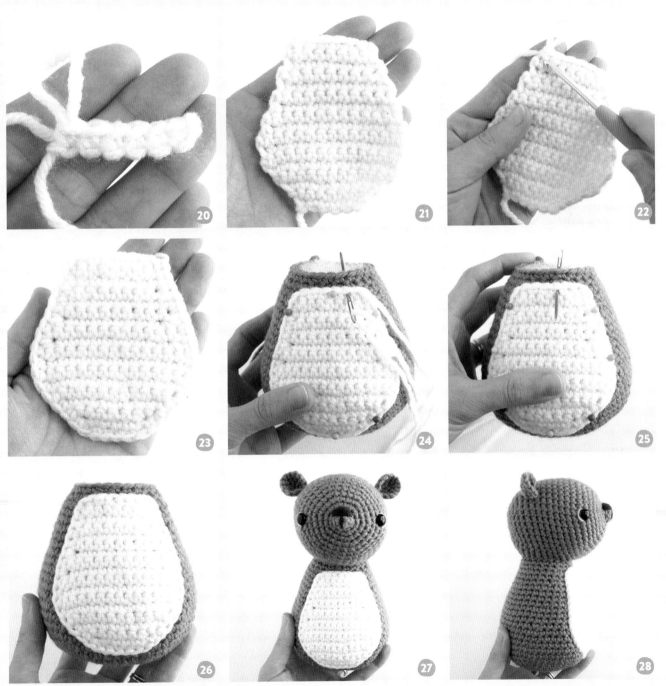

ARMS: MAKE 2

Using light brown yarn,

R1   6 sc in magic ring. (6 sts)
R2   Inc in each st around. (12 sts)
R3   Sc 12.
R4   *Sc 1, inv dec* 4 times. (8 sts)

Begin adding fiberfill and continue adding as you work the piece.

R5-12   Sc 8.
R13   Sc 3. Do this by lining up the stitches on both sides of the arm, then inserting the hook into both stitches. Then sc as normal. (photos 29-32)

Fasten off and leave a tail for sewing. (photo 33)

Using straight pins, pin the arms to the sides of the body between rounds 21-24. Make sure to pin the arms at a slight angle. With the yarn needle and the tail, sew the arms to the body. Weave the needle under both loops (the "V") from R13 of the arms and then into the body. (photo 34) Secure with a knot and hide inside the body. (photos 35-37)

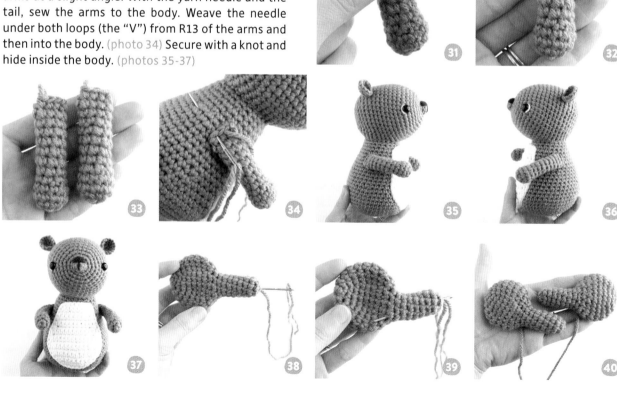

LEGS: MAKE 2

Using light brown yarn,

R1	6 sc in magic ring. (6 sts)
R2	Inc in each st around. (12 sts)
R3	*Sc 1, inc* 6 times. (18 sts)
R4	*Sc 2, inc* 6 times. (24 sts)
R5-7	Sc 24.
R8	*Sc 2, inv dec* 6 times. (18 sts)
R9	*Sc 1, inv dec* 6 times. (12 sts)
R10	Sc 3, inv dec 3 times, sc 3. (9 sts)
R11-17	Sc 9.

Add fiberfill to rounds 11-17 only, leaving the thigh unstuffed.

R18	Sc 1, inv dec 4 times. (5 sts)

Fasten off and leave a tail to close the piece. After closing the piece, weave the tail through the leg and come out near round 10. (photos 38-40)

Using straight pins, pin the legs to the sides of the body between rounds 8-16. (photos 41+42) With the yarn needle and the tail, sew the thigh to the body. The thigh will mold to the shape of the body since it is not stuffed with fiberfill. Sew around the edge of the thigh, going from the bottom to the top of the thigh. The left leg will be stitched on going counterclockwise and the right leg will be stitched on going clockwise.

Weave the needle into a stitch hole on the body, then come back through the same stitch hole and come out through one of the stitch holes on the leg. Insert the needle into the same stitch hole and go back into the body. (photos 43-45) Repeat until all of the thigh is sewn onto the body. Leave the leg, rounds 11-18, unsewn. Secure with a knot and hide inside the body. (photos 46-48)

TAIL

Using light brown yarn,

R1	6 sc in magic ring. (6 sts)
R2	Inc in each st around. (12 sts)
R3	*Sc 1, inc* 6 times. (18 sts)
R4	*Sc 2, inc* 6 times. (24 sts)
R5	*Sc 3, inc* 6 times. (30 sts)
R6	*Sc 4, inc* 6 times. (36 sts)
R7-11	Sc 36.
R12	Sc 12, inv dec 6 times, sc 12. (30 sts)
R13	Sc 9, inv dec 6 times, sc 9. (24 sts)
R14	Sc 8, inv dec 4 times, sc 8. (20 sts)

Begin adding fiberfill and continue adding as you work the piece. Leave the last couple of rounds unstuffed so the bottom of the tail can lay flat against the body.

R15-33	Sc 20.
R34	Sc 9. Do this by lining up the stitches on both sides of the tail, then inserting the hook into both stitches. Then sc as normal. (photos 49-52)

Fasten off and leave a tail for sewing. (photo 53)

Optional: Use a pet slicker brush to make the tail fuzzy. Do this before attaching the tail to the body. Hold the tail upside down and brush in the direction towards the top of the tail. (photos 54+55)

Using straight pins, pin the tail to the body near round 8. With the yarn needle and the tail, sew the tail to the body. Weave the needle under both loops (the "V") from R34 of the tail and then into the body. (photo 56) Then take the needle and sew rounds 26-33 of the tail to the body. (photo 57) Do this on both sides of the tail. Secure with a knot and hide inside the body. (photos 58+59)

172

SQUIRREL

49

50

51

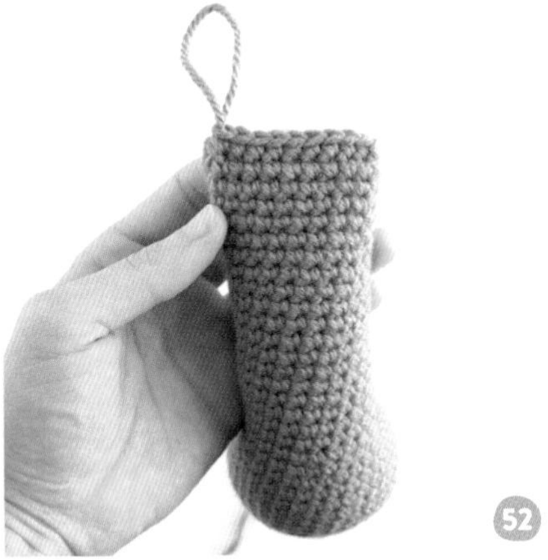
52

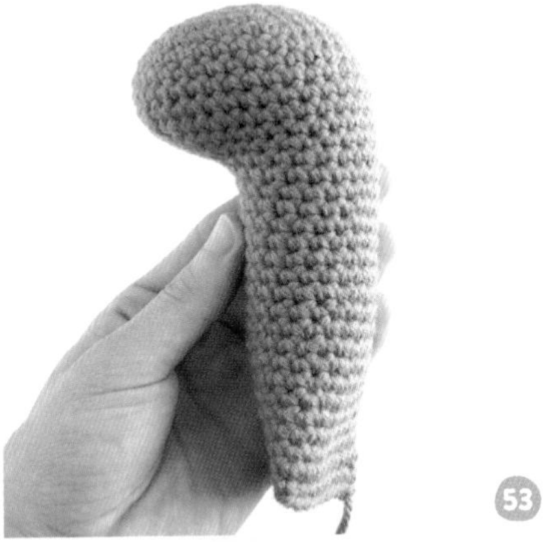
53

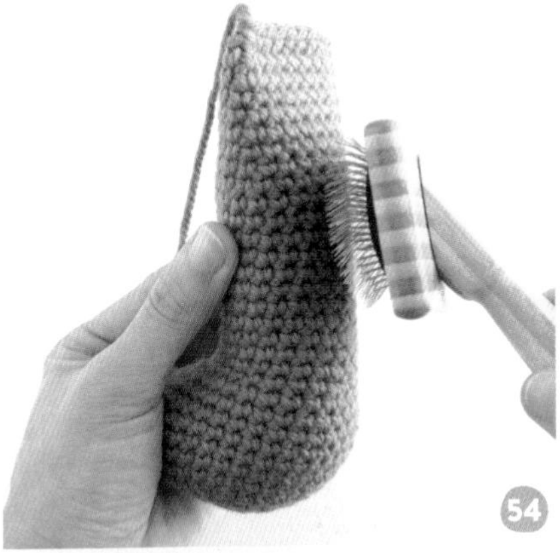
54

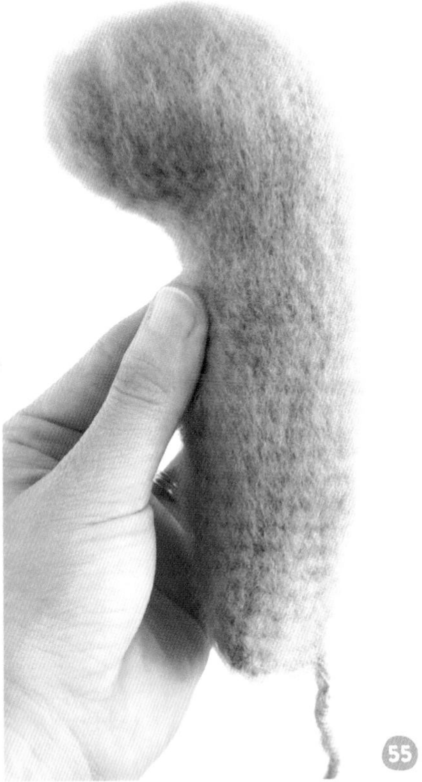
55

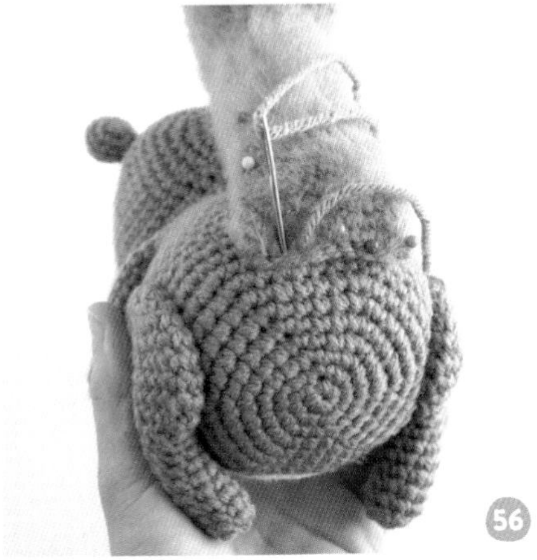
56

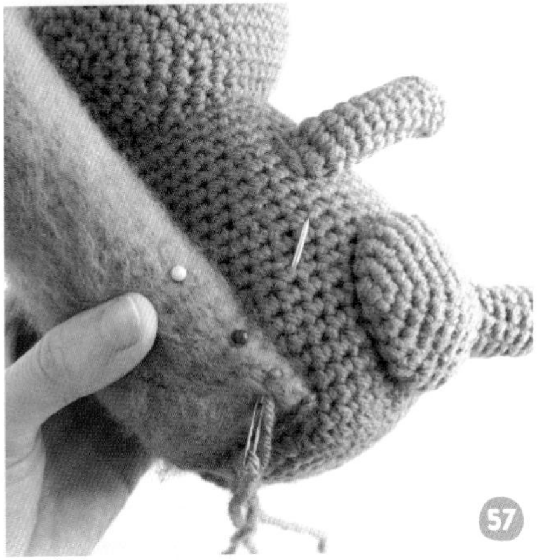
57

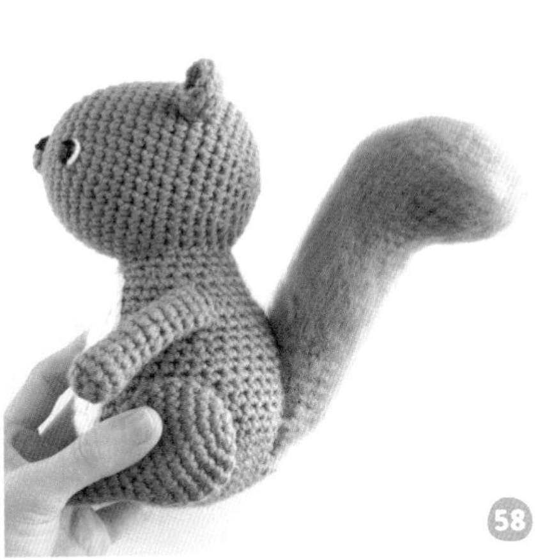
58

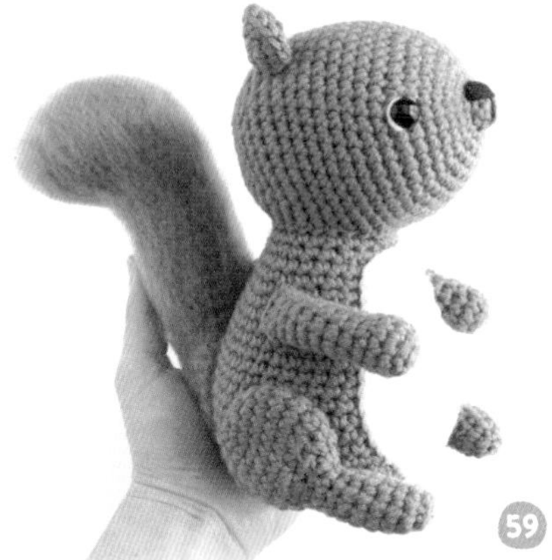
59

ACKNOWLEDGMENTS

I'm beyond grateful for all the people who helped make this book possible. Without their support, this book would still be just an idea on paper.

A massive thank you to Lindsay, Clare, Peter, Brenna, Megan, and the entire team at Blue Star Press. It's always an honor to work with all of you on these books. I'm so appreciative of the opportunity to share my work within these pages that you helped create. Thank you for constantly believing in me, for being flexible when I needed more time, and for cheering me on during every step of writing this book.

To my incredible tech editor Carmen Nuland. I can't thank you enough for investing so much of your time in making sure these patterns were accurate and as perfect as can be. Your attention to detail and thoughtful insight has helped me create another book I am so proud of.

I had the great pleasure of working with an amazing group of pattern testers for these patterns. Abby Dalager, Andrea Thiessen, Anika Kam, Anna Hall, Anna Turek, Bianca Flatman, Christina Marie, Deidra Montalvo, Elizabeth Joersz, Eswen Fava, Jason Knop, Jenessa Davis, Lysa Rohrer, Megan Bopp, Melissa Pegan, Stephanie Cothran, Tina Shunk. Thank you for sharing not only your time and feedback with me, but also your talent. Seeing each of you create these animals during testing truly made for an unforgettable experience.

I wouldn't be where I am today without my loyal and supportive followers. When I announced I was writing my third book, your enthusiasm pushed me to design my best work yet. Every like, share, message, and purchase does not go unseen, and I couldn't be more appreciative of your support. It brings me so much joy and honor to know that some of you are picking up this book and learning to crochet from it. You are what keeps me pursuing this dream of being a crochet designer.

I could never express how much I appreciate my family and all the encouragement they've given me over the years. To Rachael, Taylor, Jessica, Jacob, Grandpa, and my in-laws, Amy and George. Thank you for being on the sidelines cheering me on as I wrote this book. Getting to share these designs with you before anyone else saw them will always be my favorite memory.

To my mom and grandma, who are with me in spirit. Mom, I remember talking about this book with you when it was just an idea. I know you would have been so excited to see each animal as I finished them. I miss you every day and will be forever grateful for all the sacrifices you made and the support you always gave me. Grandma, you have played the most important role in my entire crochet career. If it wasn't for your generous heart, I wouldn't have fallen in love with crochet. You would have been tickled pink to see my books at our favorite craft store. I owe so much of my success to you.

Last but certainly not least, I want to thank my husband, Carl. You have blessed me in more ways than you will ever know. From day one you have been there to support me. You have always encouraged me to chase my dreams and are there with me every step of the way. Even on the days where all I want to do is give up. Thank you for listening to my crazy ideas (and for giving me your crazy ideas!), for being so patient with me, and for being an extra pair of hands when I needed help. I'm so incredibly lucky to have you and our pups, Thunder and Storm, by my side. Love you forever, Carl!

Published by Blue Star Press
PO Box 8835, Bend, OR 97708
contact@bluestarpress.com
www.bluestarpress.com

Photography and writing by Lauren Espy
Website: www.amenagerieofstitches.com
Instagram: @amenagerieofstitches

Cover Design by Megan Kesting
Interior Design by Rhoda Wong

ISBN: 9781950968602

Printed in COLOMBIA

10 9 8 7 6 5 4 3 2 1